Focused & Fearless:
7 Skills to Empower
Your Life

First Edition 2019

Visit: www.CharityLighten.com

LinkedIn: Charity Lighten

Twitter: Charity Lighten

YouTube: Charity Lighten

Instagram: @avibrantlife

Facebook: @avibrantlife

For information about special discounts for bulk purchases, please visit www.charitylighten.com.

To my parents who taught me about God and set me on the path to be whatever I wanted to be. To Lawson, Liberty, Saylor and Stone - you are my greatest joy, and my most important purpose - you make your mama proud! And to my husband. My love. The man who gave me the life of my dreams and taught me that we only get one shot in this life. My companion forever and very best friend. Praying for more time.

Preface

"This isn't a dress rehearsal; it isn't a dry run; it isn't a pre-performance routine. This is it. This is real life. Don't wait. Savor every minute." -*J.R. Holland*

I am drawn to people who are successfully living their best life. I love watching them, admiring them, both up close and from afar—those people that seem to be doing the savoring and have a twinkle in their eye and a bounce in their step. I love asking questions and making inquiries as to the way that they found, and are living, their best life.

In my observations, I have discovered something as unexpected as it is profound: the characteristics of so many successful leaders are not inherent personality traits or what could be labeled God-given talents. Sure, some of them are naturally gifted, and others are unquestionably naturally talented in certain areas. But beyond that, the common thread that links their life stories is that they all had put in the EFFORT and honed the SKILLS that catapulted their success. And the biggest difference between talent and skill is that one can be LEARNED.

This book is about identifying and developing those skills. I have distilled them into seven important categories: Vision, Building Resilience, Harnessing Hope, Committing to Connecting, Embracing Change, Knowing the E.N.E.M.Y, and Becoming a Multiplier.

Over the years I have witnessed what almost seems to be two completely different types of people. There are those that seem laser focused on where they are going, they seem to be filled with an infectious "joie de vivre," and they seem to have learned the secrets to create the life that they want. Then there is the other group. People in this category seem to fall on the opposite side of the spectrum. They are simply passing through life, while life is passing them by. At best they are content enough with life (things are "fine"), and at worst they struggle to even see the point of getting out of bed in the morning. This is a spectrum, and it's possible that you may have even experienced both sides at different times in your life. But what if you had the skills to become the captain of your own ship? What if just a few simple tools gave you the power to build a fearless life of meaning and purpose?

I am convinced that the seven skills outlined in this book are available to all of us and that developing them will help us lift the fogginess of life and reveal the path to living our best lives. We need more leaders. We need less fear. We need more people that are actively pursuing a life of purpose and less people disengaging from it. My hope for you is that you will dream more, do more, love more, learn more and become more. As you do, not only will your own life be blessed, but the influence that will penetrate from your actions will make this world a better place.

We all have a tendency to look at the world through the only perspective that we've ever known—our own. I am no different. And so I write this book through the many different lenses that I have worn. As a wife, I write this book for anyone in a committed relationship and I share some of my experiences and the lessons that have helped me in that role. As a mother, I write for any parent out there looking to find ways to improve things in your home. As a mother to now-teenagers, I also write this book to all of the incredible teens out there struggling to make their way in this world. In some ways your journey is one of the toughest, and who you become today can shape the rest of your life.

As an entrepreneur, business woman, and CEO of a growing brand, I also write this book from the perspective of the workplace. The 7 skills that I discuss, while predominantly addressed from the personal standpoint, have a tremendous impact on the success of individuals, teams, and leadership within business.

While I have seen the world through so many different lenses, I do make an underlying assumption about everyone. And that assumption is that the ultimate goal for ALL people is to find purpose and happiness in this life. So I write this book for anyone and everyone that is looking to develop skills that can truly change their life. The fastest path to happiness is to live a life of abundance, doing what you came to this earth to do. The skills in this book will help you on that journey.

At the end of each chapter I'll offer tips and actionable steps that can help with your personal development. But the truth is that this journey is your own. You can find incredible sources of inspiration, motivation, and reflection, but at the end of the day this is YOUR life. You decide the outcome. So while what I offer comes from a place of compassion and experience, I can't offer you a program for your life. Only you can do that!

In the pages that follow, I offer you a piece of my heart, and a prayer of hope that you will reap the rewards of developing skills that can greatly improve your life. These words are for you. The principles are for you to take and make your own! The quotes, the stories, the messages ... it doesn't matter where or from whom they originated, what matters is how YOU can use them. In this book you'll learn a lot about me; I hope you learn a lot about you as well. I hope you will ponder your own life as you read, and that insights will come that will make these words your own.

TABLE OF CONTENTS

Chapter 1

VISION

"The only thing worse than being blind is having sight but no vision."

- Helen Keller

W hen I was 19 I fell in love. Well at least I thought it was love.

His name was Dan, he was from Denver and was a few years older than I was. I had left my home in Canada to go to university in Utah—a Canadian would say "university" and an American would say "college," but you get the picture. Our first encounter was at a Christmas dinner held for our entire apartment complex. I had been asked to be involved and while serving dinner in the food line, I had made the commitment to greet everyone by name. As Dan came through the line, I quickly asked the girl next to me his name, and then casually said "Hi, Dan," while giving him a scoop of mashed potatoes. He caught my eye a few weeks later on an ice-skating rink because he was one of the few guys who could actually skate. And being from Canada, that was a must in a mate!

We hit it off right away and it was light and fun from the very beginning. It was a welcome break from my difficult classes and my part-time job washing dishes to pay for those classes. Dan had a love for life that I was drawn to. He had a spontaneous and carefree way about him that was quite the contrast from my I-like-everything-planned-out personality.

We were inseparable and it was fun and easy. Until it wasn't.

Commitment came knocking and I wasn't ready. I was young and unsure of what I wanted. I had just finished the first half of my sophomore year and I was barely feeling like I was getting my feet under me. I had been ill-prepared for many of the challenges that came from living over 2,000 miles from home, along with the financial burden of being on my own. I had fallen in love, but I was scared and wasn't ready for marriage.

He asked. I declined.

And so, I left … broken-hearted that the fun was over. And that was the end of it.

Until it wasn't.

One night he tracked me down at work. He cautiously asked me to meet him that night at the park—so we could talk.

And this is where VISION changed my life.

We met around 9 o'clock that night and sat on the merry-go-round of a now empty park. He said that he had a few things on his mind and then he did something he had never done before. He voiced his vision. And that vision included me!

He told me of our beautiful wedding, and an amazing honeymoon in Hawaii. He told me of our college graduations and starting a family—7 kids maybe. He told me of bedtime stories and star-gazing on the trampoline with Ben & Jerry's (when we could afford it someday). He offered to provide a life for me and to support me in all of my dreams. He told me of our first home and family vacations. With his words he painted a life of happiness that I could not have possibly dreamed on my own. You see, I'm not really a dreamer. But he is. And he invited me to be a part of it. In that moment, I could actually SEE and FEEL what our life would be like together … and it was INCREDIBLE!

Six days later he asked again, this time with a ring. I said yes and it's the best decision I ever made.

Vision changed the course of my future and is one of the most important skills that we can develop (which is why it earned the number one spot).

Regardless of where you are right now, vision will dictate where you are headed. I always knew that I wanted to get married, have children, and be a hands-on mom. It took me a minute to see the opportunity when it was right in front of me, but it had always been a part of my future. I remember sitting in church as a young girl doodling my wedding dress over and over. I remember writing a list as a teenager of the top 10 things I was looking for in a husband (ambition and humor were at the top). I often thought of my future life and wondered what it would be like. My point is, that without even being aware of it, I had already begun shaping my future through vision. Luckily Dan was everything I never knew I always needed!

Gusto & Guidance

We need vision for two reasons. The first is that vision is the spice of life. It adds the flavor to life that so many people seem to be missing. It's the sizzle, it's the zeal, it's the pep in our step, it's the fire in our belly. Without vision life loses its luster and loses its meaning. Knowing who we are, why we are here, and how we can contribute to this world adds purpose and excitement to life. Without it life becomes dull, mundane, and almost unbearable ... because what would be the point?

The second reason for vision is that it keeps us moving forward. It offers us the direction and allows us to put our foot on the gas. Inevitably, when we don't know where we are going, we are most likely to go nowhere at all. So we stay put. You might wonder what's so wrong with that? Comfy and cozy sound just right. The problem is that our souls crave progress, growth, learning, expanding. It's part of what makes us tick. We are creatures of untapped potential, and that potential doesn't want to be ignored. When attended to, that yearning within will direct us to some of the greatest joys in life. Some of the sweetest moments and priceless occasions will come from growth and "becoming".

Having vision is a non-negotiable; it's a "must" in terms of living fearlessly and living intentionally. Vision is what gives us the focus our lives need in order to always stay anchored to who we want to become and how we want to live. Don't ever underestimate the power of your vision to change the world. Whether that world is your home, your neighborhood, your circle of influence, or even a global movement, you must have a core belief that what you contribute can have a significant impact on the world for good.

Personal Vision

No matter what your stage of life, continuously molding your vision is a skill that can bring more happiness than almost any other. Knowing who you are and where you are going allows you to take control of your own destiny and all this world has to offer. It allows you to ACT rather than to be ACTED UPON. We don't get to control every element on our path (which is why you'll need to develop Skill #2), but we certainly get to decide how we are going to respond to life's ups and downs.

The word vision means "I know what I see." When you look at who you are and who you are becoming, do you know what you see? How do you envision your day today? Right now, as you're reading this, think back on your day (or the previous day) and evaluate where you spent your time? Was it in line with who you want to be and where you see your life going? Look back on your week and then on your month and take the time to "check-in" with yourself? Some people look to a life coach or mentor to help them stay on track, but the truth is, a little self-evaluation can go a long way. Living a life of meaning and purpose comes from aligning our hearts with our behaviors. Simply ask yourself if your day-to-day decisions are leading you to the future that you want.

It might not need to be said, but just in case you need the reminder, you must be able to imagine where you are going. If you have the tendency to think "Oh I just couldn't imagine myself doing that", or "I could never imagine being able to afford that," then it's likely you never will. You must start visualizing exactly what you want. How does it feel? What does it look like, sound like, smell like?! These feelings are the ones that will give you the reasons to continue on your path. Clinging to these "why's" will give you the motivation. How does it feel to pay off your house? How does it feel to surprise your kids with a trip to Disneyland? How does it feel to put the hurt away and hug the person you thought you could never forgive? How does it feel to get the job you've always wanted? How does it feel to hit your sales goals? Your brain is wired to take direction from your thoughts and your feelings. You must be able to imagine it before you can become it.

Reverse Engineering

What has stopped you from honing in on a clear vision for your life? Sometimes we can see where we want to go, but we aren't exactly sure how to get there. In situations like these it helps to work backwards rather than forwards. Looking at the future goal and working back one step at a time to get to the present. This can give us a better look at the pathway in front of us. I learned this exact lesson when I was a teenager.

When I was 17 I thought that holding hands on a rollercoaster at night was just about the most romantic thing imaginable. I have no clue where that idea came from, but once it hit, it was stuck for good. And I wanted it! I didn't have a boyfriend at the time, which funny enough, didn't seem to dissuade me (truthfully, I think I was more in love with the thought of the overall experience than with any particular boy). What can I say, I was a hopeless romantic back then!

The problem was that there were no roller coasters in my town. In fact, the closest roller coaster was five hours away at an amusement park in Toronto—Canada's Wonderland. Having been there once as a youth, I was pretty sure it was the happiest place on earth.

I knew that I wanted to go back … at night … with a boy. But I wasn't entirely sure how to get there.

The first thing to consider was that I didn't want to go with my family. Going with a big group of friends was way more appealing. And the bigger the group, the more likely that I would find a boy willing to participate in my adventure.

Getting there was going to be the biggest hurdle. I didn't think that my parents would let me drive five hours, spend the day enjoying the fun of an amusement park, and then drive five hours home. I pondered and mused and was convinced that there had to be a way. So I got out the yellow pages (yes, it's hard to believe there was an existence before Google) and I flipped to the bus section. I called Greyhound about their schedule, but unfortunately there were no buses that would leave and come back on the same day. But an ad in the phone book caught my eye: "Charter Your Own Bus." What?! I had no idea what charter meant, but my instincts told me that I was heading in the right direction.

I called the number and was astounded to find out that you could rent a bus AND a driver! And on top of that, you could decide when to leave and when to return. My mind was reeling! This was perfect! I got out a notebook and proceeded to call every single bus service listed in my city! I wrote down the prices for each bus along with how many seats were on the bus and quickly narrowed down the cheapest option. It was still expensive and way more money than I could even dream of scraping together. But what if I were able to fill every seat on the bus? I did the math and suddenly the numbers looked promising. I dreamt about it all night wondering how much kids would pay for some independence from their parents and a fun-filled day! I certainly didn't have a lot of extra money, so I knew the price had to be right.

The next day I called Canada's Wonderland to check on ticket prices. Back then, just like today, big amusement parks weren't chump change. A single ticket was pricey. But I talked my way through and was able to secure a fantastic price—but it required committing to a lot of tickets. I would need to fill the bus.

I now had a plan. I had a bus, I had tickets, and I quickly figured out a date that I thought would accommodate the most kids my age. It never dawned on me to try to make a profit, I just wanted to fill the bus and have a great adventure and I knew I needed to enlist others in order to make that happen.

And so I got to work.

I printed fliers and handed them out to my peers at work and at school. I spoke to everyone that I could think of and told them to tell their friends. I sold them on the dream of leaving our parents behind and enjoying some freedom at the greatest place on earth (or in Canada at least). I had no idea what FOMO was back then, but I learned that it was a big seller and I convinced many that there would be nothing worse than missing out on this experience! Fear of Missing Out is real—especially to a group of teenagers with the promise of being with the opposite sex for the day! And so little by little, one ticket at a time, with an envelope full of cash, the seats were filled, and I chartered my first bus. And it all started with a vision. Oh, and in case you're wondering, mission accomplished. I worked at McDonald's at the time and there was a boy that had been flirting with me for weeks (or maybe it was the other way around :). Luckily, he purchased a ticket, and luckily a little touching and teasing on the bus led to hand holding on the roller coaster. It was just as romantic as I had expected it to be!

Surround Yourself

If vision doesn't come easily to you and if you aren't a person that naturally dreams big, then surround yourself with people that do. Find the people that have been ignited by life and allow them to rekindle the spark that is in you. Truthfully, I am not a dreamer. I can't really pinpoint why. I'm ambitious, and I work hard, but big, grand, lofty dreams were never really my forte. For many years I struggled with scarcity thinking, and I felt that for some reason dreaming big meant that I was unappreciative of what I already had. I worried that reaching for more meant that I was being ungrateful with what I had been given and that I just needed to learn to be content with what I had. I also believed (falsely) that because I had been so blessed in my life, that somehow having more meant taking from those that had less. (More on that with Skill #7).

Meeting Dan was one of the best things that ever happened to me, for many reasons, but the one that stands out is because he's a dreamer. He thinks bigger than almost anyone I know, and he doesn't ever focus on the things that could hinder his dreams. He has a contagious way of looking at the world and not seeing any limits in life. I on the other hand notice all the limits, assess them, categorize them, rank them, and file them on a spreadsheet that I eagerly present to him by 5pm the same day. We were meant for each other haha!

Being around people that believe that anything is possible is exhilarating and they inspire us to reach for more. They push us to bigger heights, with better views and greater vistas. Sometimes their example gives us the permission we needed to become who we've always wanted to be. For so many years I was looking for permission. I was so afraid of getting on the wrong path and of disappointing God that I allowed fear to cripple me. I needed permission to fail, and I needed permission to succeed. So if that's you, and if you need someone to give you permission, then let it be me. No one has the power to keep you from your dreams except you! If no one has ever told you that you have the right to live your very best life, then hear me loud and clear! You were put on this planet to reach your highest potential, to dream big, to live with intention, and to work as hard as you can to lift others and to find joy! So don't look back. Just keep pressing forward. This world needs more people living a life of purpose. This world needs YOU!!

It's the Little Things

For many of us, living a life of purpose is directly influenced by our beliefs and core values. More often than not, these beliefs and values were shaped by the home and family (or lack thereof) that we grew up in. When I met Dan, he was very open about how much he loved kids and how important family was to him (which was one of the many things that I was attracted to). After we married we didn't wait long, and three weeks after I graduated with an accounting degree I gave birth to our first child. He was such an angel-baby that we decided to have another right away, a daughter who gave us a run for our money in the beginning. By the time I was 28, my oldest was 6 years old and we had two boys and two girls (the lottery winning combination if you ask me).

The next decade was what I lovingly refer to as the "foggy years." We were young, we were poor, and truthfully I wasn't really sure what I was doing! Dan worked hard to provide for the family, and I spent my time chasing around little kids, wondering if my mothering would cause them to need therapy some day! I worried constantly about all the things that I wasn't doing "right," and it felt like guilt was my constant companion. Were we teaching them enough, were they smart enough, were they athletic enough, did we give them enough one-on-one time?

15

The feelings of inadequacy were heavy.

One day I decided to go to a class all about family traditions. This was another area that I felt like we had failed. As I mentioned, Dan is more of a spontaneous spirit, so often our holidays looked different than the one before. As the class began, I quickly realized that I didn't have one family tradition that I could think of.

As the teacher began, I was hopeful that he would give me a list of traditions that I could then rush home and try to implement on my unsuspecting family. I was sure that this would make me feel like "Supermom." But the class wasn't really what I expected. We didn't really talk about traditions in the traditional sense, as much as we discussed the sorts of things that we consciously or subconsciously value. And that these values will emit themselves both intentionally and sometime unintentionally in our families. I gave myself a challenge to go home and try to discover the hidden messages I was sending my children.

We gathered together as a family, brought out a large poster board and a black marker. We asked the kids to list any "family traditions" they could think of, or even things that we did regularly as a family. It was slow and simple at first—"family dinner," "Saturday chores," "camping on Memorial Day weekend with all the Lightens"—and then little by little the list became quite lengthy. I may have shed a tear or two

16

as I discovered that through this list we could "see" the family I had always envisioned.

Hard work was definitely on the list. Both Dan and I valued work and we wanted to instill that in our children. One year we decided that the kids needed to have a little more responsibility, so we went out and bought chickens. Giving the chickens food and water, along with collecting eggs, became a "tradition" (and incidentally became my youngest son's first "business"—finding customers and delivering eggs each week). We later bought two goats (not for any real reason other than the added responsibility), and we kept these around much longer than the two "ducks" that Dan once brought home that grew to actually be very large geese!

We also wanted our children to know that family was important and we were glad to see that they added our weekly family nights, trips to Canada, and Grandma's yearly Halloween party to our tradition poster. One-on-one date nights, and rides in Dad's Mustang also made the list. These activities were not very frequent, but we were surprised and pleased to see that they had made such an impact.

Teaching them about faith, and trust in God, also peeked through, as they asked if "going to church" and "family prayer" counted as traditions. "What about feeding the homeless?" one of them asked. We had only done this once at the time, but it was a reminder to me that I wanted my children to be aware of others in need and was so glad it made it onto our list (which forced us to keep it up ever since).

This was a special night for me, as I began to see that the vision I thought I had failed to share with my children was actually present and quite apparent. Sure, there were plenty of times when the kids fought like crazy, when dinner was frozen burritos, when I lost my temper and raised my voice, when the bank accounts were empty, when I put myself in time-out just to get away from them, or when Dan and I didn't get along. But overall, this little activity helped me see the vision that we had created.

Our life is a culmination both of who we are (our character) and the little things that we do each day. Our routines are derived from the things that are important to us, and the things that are important to us should be reflected in the "routines" of our life. When my kids were little I didn't think I had a clear picture of where we were going, but in looking back, it was the little things that we did each day that allowed me to see that our vision and our actions were aligned (most of the time). If you want to see where you are going, simply take a look at the direction you are heading. And I don't mean that to be a cliché at all. Seriously look at where you are heading. What are the little things that you do frequently? How do you spend your time? If you want to be a great salesperson, what steps are you taking each day to hone the craft of salesmanship? If you want to lose weight, what are the daily things that you are doing to make advancement in that area? If you want a killer marriage, what does that daily effort look like for you? It's the little things that count the most, but often feel too insignificant to be worthy of our attention. These are the building blocks of your life! These are the little things that will incrementally add to the picture that you want to paint for your life! Each stroke, combined consistently over time, will reflect the masterpiece that's already inside of you.

Lead By Example

Finding your vision and sharing it with others can be life changing. But just as sure as positive experiences can come, so too can the negative ones. We all know the saying, "misery likes company," and bad habits can be just as magnetic as good ones. People are watching you. Right now, in your life, I promise that there are people that are being influenced and shaped by the decisions YOU are making. Depending on who you are, and what you do, this group may be big or small. The size doesn't matter but the impact does. I think of those who struggle with body image, and the message that this sends to others. I think of those who have bad tempers, the over spenders, the pessimists, the worriers, the complainers, or whatever other bad habits that may inadvertently give others permission to follow in our footsteps. I have seen some of my own shortcomings show up in my children and it makes me want to recommit to doing just a little better. People are always watching, so be aware of the example you are setting.

Michael Wilcox is an incredible professor I had in college. He shared a story with me that I will never forget. His teenage summers were spent on his uncle's ranch. He had one job to do and he hated it. Mending fences. Cows aren't the smartest of creatures and his job could attest to that. The grazing cows would often see the green grass on the other side of the wire fences, and just as the saying goes, thought it looked a little greener. And so the large cows would nuzzle their heads through the fence and work mightily to get their shoulders through in order for them to graze on the new grass. Thinking nothing of their actions, they would eat until full and then be on their way. The fences were designed to keep the large cows in, but the newly formed gaps that they created with their upper bodies created a danger zone for those that they least expected. Their calves. Only the calves were small enough to fit through the holes in the fences, and the calves were the ones to break through and get lost, all due to following the examples set before them.

The choices that we make are likely to affect people within our circle of influence. In some regards you could say that private choices are not really that private; they all have public consequences. A world leader once said, "The public cost in human life and tax dollars for these so-called private choices is enormous: poverty, crime, a less-educated workforce, and mounting demands for government spending to fix problems that cannot be fixed by money. It simply is not true that our private conduct is our own business. Our society is the sum total of what millions of individuals do in their private lives. That sum total of private behavior has worldwide public consequences of enormous magnitude. There are no completely private choices."

Are you leading the way you were meant to lead? Are you confidently forging a path that others can safely follow? People are drawn to those who know where they are going. People crave direction, confidence, courage, and leadership. Whether you've chosen it or not, there will always be those who look to you for guidance and leadership. You have an influence, so use it for good!

Vision in Leadership

If you are the CEO of a Fortune 500 company or the leader of a startup, if you are the head of a congregation or your school choir—don't underestimate the power of vision. Great leaders have vision.

To quote one of the greats, "companies live or die on leadership." If you are a leader, don't assume your vision is understood by others. Don't assume that people have your passion or can see the direction you are heading. How are you sharing your vision? How are you motivating with it? If you know where you want to go, do you know the steps it takes to get there?

One of the most memorable leaders of our time was John Fitzgerald Kennedy. As president of the United States, he inspired generations with his speeches and fearlessly shared the vision he had for this country. That vision included a country where skin color would not disqualify you for basic human decency, a country where individuals with disabilities could still find opportunity, and a country where one day man would walk on the moon.

President Kennedy was just months into his presidency in 1961 when he challenged America's space scientists to up their game and get the first man to the moon by the end of the decade. Not the end of the century. The decade! It was an audacious request at the time. The Soviet Union was way ahead in the space race. It had placed the first satellite in the upper atmosphere three years earlier and had already successfully sent the first person to orbit the earth. No one was betting on America to be first to the moon. But this didn't stop JFK. He encouraged others with his famous "moon speech," saying, "We choose to go to the moon in this decade and do the other things, not because they are easy, but because they are hard".

We recently went to Texas, and as we toured the International Space Center and saw one of the massive rockets on display, I was truly in awe of what had been accomplished. (I may have also embarrassed Dan by shouting, "Woah! We've been to the moon more than once?!" ... how was I supposed to know?) JFK wasn't the first man to stand on the moon, but if it hadn't been for his vision, it's safe to say that Neil Armstrong would never have taken his "one small step for man, one giant leap for mankind." He had confidence in the space program and that confidence led to one of the most historical events of all time.

Being Present

There is a lot of talk these days about "staying present," "living in the moment," and being more aware. To me this is the perfect complement, and not the antagonist, of vision. Staying present means fighting against distraction, which is the enemy to both living for "now" and for the future (more on the enemy in Chapter 6). It means living intentionally and "on purpose," so that you don't ever look back and wonder how in the world you got there.

Part of living your very best life is the ability to savor every moment. To celebrate successes both small and large along your journey. Mindfulness, meditation, and intentional consciousness are all tools that help us

23

to stop and savor. To briefly pause and simply "see." It allows us to analyze the path that we are on, and gives us cause to celebrate how far we have come. This precise revelry is the fuel that rekindles our commitment to plan, prepare and propel forward on our pilgrimage through life. Making time to halt, and take a respite from life, offers proof to ourselves that we are active participants in our own stories. Staying present allows us to redirect, rededicate, and recommit to the life that we seek.

Stay the Course

Having vision does not necessarily mean that you know the beginning from the end, and it certainly doesn't mean that life will take you in a direct course. If you talked to 100 people and asked them what they thought they would be when they grew up, it's likely that 90% of them would say they are doing something completely different than they had thought (keep in mind that 62% of all statistics are made up on the spot :). Having vision means you are always looking forward, while at the same time checking in with where you are right now. Only you will know where you're going. Only you will know when it's time to make a shift. Stay true to the music inside of you. You have unique gifts, talents, and perspectives that will guide you on your journey. You may have thoughts, inklings, ideas or a blurry picture of your future, but a picture nonetheless. Stay true to that. As you set your path, always stay in tune with your own intuition. It will lead you to where you need to go.

By the time I had three little kids, I started to feel a little nagging in my brain. I've always had an entrepreneurial spirit and it started to call out to me. We had purchased our first home, I was starting to get the hang of the whole motherhood thing, and I was anxious to put some of my talents to use. I told Dan that I wanted to start a little business and he was so supportive when I opened Lighten Tax Service out of the basement of our home. After doing this for a couple of years I had the courage to try something new, and I started a little eBay business. We had a Pottery Barn store in our city and I learned that if I purchased items on clearance and listed them on eBay before the same items went on sale in the catalogs that I could turn a small profit. I then did the same thing with large rugs, and pretty soon I had shipments being picked up daily. I was soon drawn to learning something new, and I began a business that involved hosting jewelry parties. I would provide the silver beads, Swarovski crystals, jewels, toggles, etc., and a hostess would invite friends and neighbors into her home to make their own bracelets, necklaces, and earrings. It was a great way for me to socialize for a few hours in the evenings and make some extra income. On top of that, I was able to hire my first two employees— it was a REAL business :) I eventually decided to sell the jewelry business in order to explore the real estate industry. I got licensed as an agent and eventually learned all about building a home. I took a leap of faith and decided to be the general contractor on our dream home. I was so daunted, but I knew I could do it. (This is the home we live in now, and luckily it just survived its first earthquake—phew).

There are other business adventures that I'll tell you about later, but my point is that each step I took led to another step. I didn't necessarily know where I was going but each door opened eventually led to another door. And the truth is that I was nervous each time. Every single time. But there was just something inside me that propelled me forward. I didn't really know where I was going until I got there, but each step ignited my passions. Our lives are often lived one step and one chapter at a time. There are different seasons, and different occasions. Vision is about staying prepared, recognizing the season, and seizing the opportunities when they come. Even when you're scared.

Finding Clarity

Vision is the fuel that drives opportunity, progress, and fulfillment. With it, we know where we've been and, most importantly, we know where we are going. If you are still scratching your head saying, "Charity, thanks for the stories and all, but I'm still not really sure that I know who I am, or where I want to go," to you I say, "Don't fret." Like all the skills in this book, finding clarity can be learned. It is not a personality trait that you are born with, rather it is something that you attain through effort and exploration. For some people a flash of inspiration might hit, but for most, figuring out what you are meant to contribute to the world will come by trying new things, asking different questions, and sorting through the many opportunities in life. Trial and error are a part of discovery. Vision will come line upon line; here a little and there a little. Deciphering your path involves personal inquisition, thoughtful experimentation, and learning more about what makes you tick. What are the things that excite you? What are you naturally good at? How does it serve others? What passions or causes pull at your conscience and your heart? What do you value and what do you hope to accomplish in life?

As you begin to build a life of purpose and happiness, pay attention to the clues on your path. Feeling invigorated and excited to learn are signs that you are heading in the right direction. Your passion will reveal itself. And don't worry, you are not lacking passion! I promise it's in you. There is something inside of you that will light right up when the circuits are flowing, when all the cylinders are firing, and when there are no blockages. It might be hiding or maybe for some reason you're trying to suppress it ... but it's there! Even if you can't see it clearly, it's there. Fear is so often what blinds us from our passion. Fear is the dark veil, the black nemesis, the complete dream killer. When you learn to quiet the doubts and conquer the fears, you'll discover inside a beautiful, immense, limitless reservoir of passion. As you pursue a life of greatness, just keep moving forward! Dig deep to remember exactly who you want to be. Knowing what you want is understanding your *why*. Put in the work. "Where" you are on your path does not matter nearly as much as simply "being" on the path. Make the effort and hold the vision of your character always in your mind's view. Clarity will come as you press onward. As Dory liked to say in *Finding Nemo,* just keep swimming.

PRACTICAL TOOLS to gain Vision:

1. **Find some QUIET TIME.** In the hustle and bustle of everyday life, this just might be the hardest thing to do. But finding time to get away from ALL distractions and check in with "what you see" is key. Who are you? What are your talents? What do you want from this life? Simply spend a little time evaluating YOURSELF. Find a time in your daily/weekly/monthly routine to visualize yourself achieving your goals. What does it look, feel, or sound like?

2. **Focus on your focus.** Make a conscious effort to see the sorts of things that you are focusing on. Write a list each week of the top five things

28

that you have spent the most time thinking about. Some may surprise you and some may be downright embarrassing. Take a look at this list and make sure your brain power is being used to guide you in the right direction. Evaluate the list and make sure you aren't giving unnecessary attention to things that will not help you grow (I'm talking to you Netflix)!

3. **Break it down**. There are likely many areas of your life that will require a little vision, so break it down into categories that are important to you. Once you have the categories, give yourself a score of 1-10 on how well you think you are doing in that category. By scoring yourself each month you will get a clearer picture of which areas are thriving and which areas might need a little more attention. Here are some that I use: Family, Finances, Friendship, Adventure, Business, Health, Spiritual, and Learning.

4. **Safe-guard your mind**. When you know where you want to go, hold on to it with both hands. Many people start with great vision, but few have the power to control what goes into their mind. We are living in an age where information, opinion, influence, and rhetoric are running rampant, and often they are running full force into our mind, completely unchecked. You MUST be the gatekeeper of

your mind. NO ONE else will do that for you. Keep out the junk, the doubt, the fear, the worry, or even the "harmless" opinions of others. They are NOT you and they do not know where you are going. You are the master of your fate - so protect the mind that will guide you there.

5. **Start your day with intention**. Set your alarm clock, get up, and then mentally prepare for the day! This might sound a little "grade-school" but one of the easiest ways to take control of your day is to decide when and how it starts. You get to decide. Every single rotation of the earth brings a new day—you don't get to decide that. But you do get to decide exactly how you want each day to begin. Develop an intentional morning routine that will help you achieve your goals. Once this is mastered, just imagine all the other things you can master.

CHAPTER 2

BUILDING RESILIENCE

"The world breaks everyone and afterwards many are strong at the broken places"

-Ernest Hemingway

D an had vision and it changed the course of my life. But he didn't ever warn me of the possible falling rocks on the road we decided to drive down together. How could he know of the challenges of raising four little kids? How could he know that one of them would be hit by a car walking home from Scouts and have us praying like never before and gratefully seeing miracles? How could he predict the financial collapse of 2008 or the even harder blow of a dishonest business partner? When he shared his vision of our beautiful life together, how could he know of the struggles that we would face? How could he possibly begin to prepare for the dark night when he would quietly pull me into our bedroom, unable to hold back the sorrow as he gently told me that, at the age of 43, he had stage 4 cancer?

There are some things that even the greatest vision can't prepare you for.

Wind & Trees

In the late 80's and early 90's, scientists constructed a research facility in Arizona called Biosphere 2. The idea was to build a controlled environment in order to better understand nature. Researchers were able to plant a variety of things in this "perfect environment" and learn from the observations. In this experiment, trees grew rapidly, but then something unexpected began to happen. The trees began to fall over. It was puzzling at first. They had adequate sunshine, the correct amount of water, and the perfect combination of nutrients in the soil. Everything that a tree would need to grow healthy and strong. Everything except the one thing the scientists hadn't accounted for: wind. In the wild, trees must withstand strong wind and as a result develop what is called stress wood – strong, fibrous wood that vastly improves the quality of life for a tree. Without the wind, the trees didn't develop the strong bark or deep roots needed for lasting survival.

We all face pain, disappointment, difficulty, and doubt. Change, hardships, troubles, and trials seem to go hand in hand with life. How do we make ourselves, our families, our businesses, and our communities wiser and stronger to rise above the difficulties and the obstacles of life? This is where the second skill of resilience becomes necessary. Resilience is the ability to "bounce back," to bend without breaking, to recover quickly, and come out on top despite life's challenges. It's being able to adapt to whatever is thrown your way—a skill that can change your life! It's getting through life stronger than you started.

With effort, focus, and intention we can build a life full of joy, meaning, and purpose, in spite of, or possibly because of, the difficulties along the way. With the right tools we can take control of our afflictions and have the capacity to overcome. One of life's great paradoxes is that struggle can build wells of strength. This does not happen automatically. For some, the struggles can be their undoing. But for others, with their intention set to face the wind, fear can be turned into courage. Injury and insult can lead to insight. Pain can give way to perseverance and weaknesses can be transformed into wisdom and strength.

Adversity will be a constant or occasional companion for each of us throughout our lives. We cannot avoid it. The question is how we will respond to it. So how do you prepare for the unexpected? How do you build a foundation strong enough to withstand the earthquakes of life? How do you build enough resiliency to come out the victor and not the victim? What steps can be taken to better prepare for the rain and the winds and the storms of life?

Recognize The Opportunities

When I left home to go to school I was young, I was naive, and I was broke. I may have been 18, but I had very few other qualities that would classify me as an adult. Nonetheless, I was excited about the adventure of living away from home, and independently navigating life. I probably should not have been quite so eager about the independent part. I really knew very little about college life and had not adequately prepared for the financial aspects. I had made two assumptions that I thought would be sufficient. The first was that I would be able to get a job to help pay the bills, and the second was that I would be able to get a student loan. Unfortunately, because of my citizenship, both would prove to be quite challenging.

Apparently, there are things like "immigration laws," "alien citizenships," and "work visas" that regulate jobs in this country ... who knew?!! When I went to apply for my first job, the application asked for a social security number. When I told the employer that I didn't have one (and didn't know what that was), he tilted his head and then hesitantly said, "Umm... then you can't work here." I eventually figured out that as a Canadian without the proper visa (a student visa wasn't sufficient), I was not allowed to legally hold a job. Luckily, I found a little loophole. Because the school I was attending was a private school, I was allowed to be employed on campus only. However, there were some restrictions. I had to first complete one semester of school, and once eligible for employment I would be limited to work 20 hours a week. I quickly did the math of 20 hours multiplied by my wage of $4.25/hour and it didn't take long to see that I was in trouble.

This brought me to my next plight of trying to get a student loan. After meeting with a financial counselor, I was devastated to learn that the student loan program offered to American citizens was NOT offered to Canadians. They gently explained that there was fear that a student would return to their native country without repaying the loan, leaving them with no recourse. The Canadian government held to the same standard, saying that the probability of me staying in the states would pose the same financial risk to them. I was denied by both countries, and my appeals fell on deaf ears.

I was devastated. I calculated what I had, and even after washing dishes during my second semester, and donating plasma each week, I would not have enough to stay in school. My sweet parents took pity on me and offered to give me a loan. I would make monthly payments and try to work it off over the summer.

I completed my freshman year of school and returned home for the summer. I had two very prestigious jobs lined up for when I arrived: McDonald's and Pizza Hut. One during the day and one on evenings and weekends. My parents and younger siblings had an opportunity to spend most of that summer in Europe, leaving me home alone for most of it. My aunt was dying, and my mother wanted the family to spend time with her and to experience where she grew up. I had little choice—it was stay home and work or forgo the next year of school.

My summer was uneventful; between working two jobs and no family around, my main goal was simply to earn money. I was nearing my financial goal when a very unfortunate event occurred. I was on my way to a one-day job handing out samples when I got into my first car accident. It was only a fender bender, but I was driving my Dad's Geo Metro (if you don't know that that is, think "tin can") and I rear ended a Cadillac. To make matters worse, my parents informed me that I would not be able to claim the accident on their insurance. I sobbed for weeks as I realized that my summer savings would be sucked up by one lousy car accident.

For years this experience was a source of bitterness for me. I felt like I had worked "so hard," and tried to do the "right things," and that the universe had served me a total injustice. Bad things weren't supposed to happen to good people, right?! I was resentful towards my parents (even though they lent me the money that I needed to continue my schooling), I was angry that my roommates didn't have to work, and I was upset about my overall "misfortune." Sadly, my bitterness to the whole situation was blinding me from seeing the valuable lessons that were shaping my life. In the moment, I didn't recognize that I was developing grit that would serve me later on in life. I was learning lessons that were crucial in getting me to where I am today. I learned how to be frugal and stretch a dollar. I learned the valuable skill of problem-solving (even if I was kicking and screaming at the time). I learned that when we feel like life is ganging up on us, it's okay to ask for help. My boyfriend at the time, and his sweet father, spent endless hours replacing parts on the Geo Metro, removing dents, buffing out dings, and repainting. To this day I worry that I didn't thank them enough. I also learned the very critical lesson of taking 100% responsibility for my own actions.

I was gaining skills that would benefit me and my future family. I was learning how to overcome hardship and developing self-confidence, empathy, and a compassion for those that struggle. Through my hardship I was experiencing firsthand some of life's challenges that would better prepare me for things to come. At the time they felt so heavy (though looking back they weren't really that hard), but I made it through each obstacle with a resilience that I could not have achieved in any other way. I also felt God echo a statement that my father said to me when I was still complaining to him a few years later. He said,

"One day you will thank me for helping to build your character." It felt quite hurtful at the time, but over the years, and through other experiences, I have learned the wisdom in those words (so thank you Dad). What doesn't kill you makes you stronger—yet another cliché that became my reality.

Life is full of ups and downs and we have a tendency to celebrate the ups and curse the downs. While the "easier times of life" should certainly be relished and enjoyed, it's the valleys of our lives that often provide the most learning and the most growth. Our purpose in life is to find both joy AND growth. Therefore, every aspect of our life, the highs and lows, ought to be appreciated for what they are! And on the days that seem oh so hard, the days when you don't think you have what it takes to get through, those are the days that you just take it one moment at a time. One step in front of the other.

There is nothing that you can't get through. Nothing.

My heart goes out to people that are hurting, especially people in pain. People that deal every single day with some sort of chronic pain. Nothing hurts my heart more or makes me feel more helpless than when I see Dan in pain. But even to you I say keep going. You can do this. You're stronger than you think.

The Science

There is no question that we are all different, and among those differences is how we handle life's challenges. We've likely all seen different examples of people who seem to crumble under even the slightest pressure, while others emerge from some of life's horrors with more strength and vigor than ever before. Ideally resiliency is something that is learned in childhood, but research shows that some people develop resilience, or the ability to overcome serious hardship, while others simply do not. So what makes some people more resilient and better able to cope than others?

There is no doubt that extreme stress and hardship in childhood—such as that caused by neglect, abuse, exposure to violence and mental illness in caregivers—can threaten the development of a child. Many studies have identified a commonality among children whose life outcomes were remarkably positive despite their exposure to a variety of adverse experiences that typically produce challenges in learning, behavior, and overall health. Findings from Harvard's Center on the Developing Child showed that the single most common factor for children who develop resilience is having at least one stable and committed relationship with a supportive parent, caregiver, or other adult. John Shonkoff, MD of the Harvard Center, says that "These relationships provide the personalized responsiveness, scaffolding,

41

and protection that buffer children from developmental disruption. They also build key capacities that enable children to respond adaptively to adversity and thrive."

While supportive relationships are critical, the science on resilience shows that there are other factors that can also help us learn how to live with ongoing fear, and give us the ability to adapt in spite of life's challenges. These factors are drawn from within and include a personal sense of control over life's circumstances; a sense of being in charge of your own fate. Other considerations involve having had opportunities to strengthen adaptive and self-regulatory skills. An example of this would be a child going to "time out" in order to learn how to calm themselves down. Additionally, resiliency is built with the support provided by faith, hope (Skill #3), and cultural traditions. Fundamentally, resilience rests on relationships, along with the ability to draw upon a variety of resources during difficult times.

Based on this list, we can rest assured that resiliency is a skill that can be learned. And it's never too late! It is absolutely possible to strengthen your inner self, to gain a belief in your personal strength, and to see yourself as completely capable of any challenge. This does not mean that we have to pretend that the affliction isn't real. We don't need to downplay the difficulty or the downright terrible. Pain is painful, stress is stressful, and healing takes time. But it means that we don't let these situations define us. It means that we understand that life may someday burn us, and we show up anyway. We strap on the boxing gloves and we step into the ring. It means we develop self-mastery (Skill #7) and we take control of our lives, and we persevere!

Confidence & Responsibility

When our children were small, I had a deep desire to instill in them self-esteem—especially my two daughters. My hope was that if they were confident in who they were then they would never have to compromise or make poor choices in order to seek approval from outside sources. My problem was that I had no clue how to ensure they had self-confidence. Was this a characteristic that people were born with, or was confidence something that could possibly be learned? I was certainly willing to offer unconditional love in hopes of "loving them into confidence," but my hunch told me there was more to it than just love.

I decided to do some research and was both surprised and encouraged by what I found. According to the experts, self-esteem can in fact be "learned," and one of the determining factors is the ability to accomplish what appear to be challenging tasks. The research shows that when challenges are overcome, children will tend to feel confident and good about themselves, leading to feelings of being capable and worthy. These "challenges" ought to be age-appropriate, and the key is making them just difficult enough to seem somewhat daunting, yet still within reach to be successfully completed.

I was excited and wanted to start right away. I looked at my small children and tried to determine the tasks that I thought they could successfully accomplish with a little effort.

That night after dinner I told my four-year-old son (my oldest) that I had a new responsibility that I thought he was ready for. It was going to be difficult, but I knew he could do it. Eager to please, he listened attentively as I told him that he was now old enough to unload the dishwasher. I watched as he excitedly began his new task. I held my breath that the large plates wouldn't end up shattered on the floor, and that he would pick up the proper side of the sharp knives. I will never forget the look of sheer confidence and accomplishment that glowed from his face when he put the last fork away and closed the dishwasher.

I felt like I was onto something and decided to assign tasks to my two daughters, a one-year-old and three-year-old. Now you might be wondering what in the world could a one-year-old, still in diapers and hardly able to talk, possibly do? I had the same thoughts and wracked my brain. Then as I was changing her diaper I wondered if she knew where the garbage was. I had never specifically pointed it out to her, but she was a bright child. When I finished changing her, I wrapped up the diaper and said, "Saylor, can you please put your diaper in the garbage?" She looked at me somewhat quizzically, and then I watched hesitantly as she took the diaper from my hand and sauntered over to the garbage. She could barely reach the cupboard handle but sure enough she reached up, opened the door and threw her diaper in the garbage. I was absolutely elated, and as I cheered and acknowledged her success, her smiling eyes filled with complete pleasure and pride!

Finding Balance

While the premise of building resilience involves strength, and a "dig-deep" attitude, there is also wisdom in only bearing what is necessary. An equally important part of resiliency is the ability to avoid undesirable stress and to harness the resources needed to sustain your well-being. Resiliency encompasses having the insight to identify the times in life that require restoring and recharging. It's true that we need to develop the strength to endure tribulation, but our capacity to persevere can be largely influenced by our ability to know when it's time to pause and refill our bucket.

I remember hearing the phrase "an inexperienced pilot will try to speed up during turbulence." Knowing very little about aviation I inquired of my brother-in-law who has his own plane. He admitted that the gut

45

reaction when hitting turbulence is to try and speed up so that you can get through it as quickly as possible. He then explained that there is an optimal speed for every phase of flight, and that with turbulence, the speed often requires slowing down and not speeding up. There is an "optimum turbulence penetration speed" that will minimize the effects of the turbulence on the aircraft, and this speed is typically slower than regular flight speed.

This is a great reminder that sometimes the turbulence in life is best handled by deliberately slowing down, rather than trying to power through. It's learning to recognize when we are approaching a breaking point, and to then make time for renewal and rejuvenation. To find ways to unwind and regroup. There are a myriad of options that help people to cope with the demands of everyday life—music, family, friends, laughter (or a good cry), a long bath, exercise, meditation, chocolate (duh), writing, reading (but not arithmetic). Travel, massage, therapy … the list can go on and on. The key is to be in tune with your own needs and to understand when it's time to amplify your efforts and when it's time to seek reprieve from the storm.

"Stressful Situations"

We wanted our four children to learn how to be okay with being uncomfortable, so we created something called "stressful situations." (To this day they will roll

46

their eyes if you even utter that phrase in their presence). Our theory was that if they could overcome difficult situations within the love and safety of our family unit, then they would be better qualified to face life's challenges on their own when the time came.

These "stressful situations" began with very simple tasks that we knew would stress them out, but we were convinced that they would develop the skills that would help them cope with the stress. Is it bad that we took a little enjoyment out of these situations? For every empty box of cereal left in the pantry, and for every "Eww, is that dinner?!" I thought a little stressful situation was harmless retaliation.

One of our daughters absolutely hated to talk to adults (she's a senior in high school now and still isn't really a fan). We knew this was a skill that would serve her well if she could successfully develop it. We began by making her checkout by herself at the grocery store and making her dentist appointments by calling the receptionist on her own. She certainly DID NOT appreciate this new form of love. On one occasion I felt like we had been slacking and that she was getting soft (like when we made her buy the tickets for a basketball game and she adamantly refused). I told her that the following Saturday she would need to ride the public transportation all by herself into downtown Salt Lake City. This was not something that she had ever done (and truthfully, we don't use our public transit very often), but this was another skill that I wanted her to have at least attempted before she left home.

Her task was to figure out how to purchase her own ticket on Traxx, take it downtown, and then get off the train. She was to take a selfie somewhere in the downtown area and then catch a separate train and return home. She was 16 at the time and had a cell phone in case there was an emergency. Needless to say, she was NOT PLEASED with me AT ALL. My son was a missionary in Brazil at the time and public transportation was his only means of getting around, and something that I quickly realized we had not prepared him for. Child #3 got the brunt of my determination and she could sense that I was not backing down. Using her ingenuity, she quickly recruited two cousins to accompany her on the journey (both mothers called with concerned inquiries about "what this was all about?"). The assigned day arrived with reluctance on her part, but luckily everything went off without a hitch. The three cousins wound up having a blast exploring the city, and an invigorating sense of new-found independence accompanied them on their way home. They were absolutely thrilled with their accomplishments and have since embarked on their own adventures throughout the state! (Though they are now begging to go alone to Hawaii for their senior trip where they will "you know, just sleep on the beach." Umm..NO!)

We all know that life can be hard! We know that unexpected trials can be lurking around the corner, but how many of us are actively preparing for these hardships? Certainly, our job as parents is to reduce our children's exposure to significant danger, but isn't our job also to give them the strength and the coping tools necessary to overcome adversity when it eventually comes? Heck, isn't it our job to be prepared OURSELVES when the hard knocks come? I felt that I was building resilience in my children, but when I decided to turn the magnifying glass onto myself, I wasn't sure I was faring so well. I was comfortable with my life at the time and wasn't keen on adding any undue stress to my own life ...but that was about to change.

Back To School

There are certain "keystone events" that happen in our lives that give us just enough of a jolt that they reset the trajectory of our lives. Almost like a small adjustment to the train track that suddenly takes you on a completely new route through life. This was the precise sort of event that occurred for me when I had a dear friend ask, "Have you ever thought of getting your master's degree?" For some reason this question rocked my core and I stumbled and stammered over the answer. "No. Of course not ... I don't know ... No. How could I possibly do that? ... I mean, of course I love learning, and that sounds intriguing ... Maybe. I probably couldn't afford it ... No. My kids need me, although they are in school all day ... No. Definitely not." With deep wisdom, so characteristic of this sweet friend, she gently prodded, "What if I could find a way to have your schooling paid for through scholarships?"

Something awoke in me that day, and suddenly I couldn't get the thought out of my head (which on a side note is often a clue that you're on the right track). I had a passion for knowledge, and always had piles of books beside my bed. At the time of this incredible offer, I was a "Food for Life Instructor" (more on that later) and was teaching healthy cooking classes, corporate lunch-and-learns, and had a small cooking segment on our local morning news. I had a passion for health and wellness and longed to learn all I could about nutrition and disease, but I had never imagined going back to school.

With fear in my mind but excitement in my heart, I nervously decided to take the leap, fully aware of the hurdles that lay ahead. One of those hurdles was that my bachelor's degree was in accounting and the master's degree I would be pursuing was in nutrition science. Yep science! When I dusted off my old transcripts and compared them to the required prerequisites, there was an obvious gap in science-based classes. It would take over a year of classes to even be able to apply to graduate school (not to mention the mandatory GRE exam).

One of those classes was organic chemistry. Oh organic chemistry, the demise of so many dreams among so many aspiring students. This was the just beginning of my education as an adult, and I was determined to spend as little money as possible on the prerequisites. I did my research and found a reputable school in California that offered an online organic chemistry class that would be accepted by Tufts (my graduate school of choice). I scoured online forums of students that had completed the class and found blazing red flags! Although the class was indeed one of the cheaper options, apparently the final exam was a beast. Multiple warnings shouted that the exam was brutal, and that regardless of your standing in the class come the final, a grade of less than 70% would be an automatic fail in the class. I had always been a pretty good student, so I wasn't fazed too badly. Big mistake.

I began the class in the spring and was pleasantly surprised by my new-found love of science. I had to get used to the "independent study" (I mean COMPLETELY INDEPENDENT...and since my mother taught me that if you can't say something nice, then don't say anything at all, I will leave both the professor and the school unnamed), but overall I was doing well. Quite well. In fact, by time the final exam rolled around I had a 96% in the class and was feeling pretty confident. Another mistake.

When it came time to take the final exam, I drove to the testing center, allowing myself plenty of time before I would need to pick up the kids from school. I walked into the test a confident woman and came out a complete mess. The exam was hard. Brutally hard! I mustered my way through it and felt somewhat uncertain in some areas and completely lost in others. I went over it again and again, and there was no real way of knowing how I did. I would simply have to wait for the results.

The timing happening to be the first days of summer and marked the final days of school for our children. We had decided to embark on a cross country adventure as a family. We rented a large motorhome and planned to spend a week on the road, discovering new sites and states along the way. I had been teaching quite a few classes, and between those, being in school, planning our vacation, and the day-to-day rigors of being a wife and mother, I was ready for a break. I was feeling quite burned out and was looking forward to a fun week with my favorite people. I tried to put the thoughts of the exam out of my mind, and simply enjoy the summer.

We had a memorable time as a family and I highly recommend touring the country by motorhome. We were heading home, and things were going wonderfully, the kids were all getting along, and spirits were high. I woke up early that morning to see the email in my inbox that I had been anticipating. Nervously, I took a deep breath. "You can do this, I told myself." I opened the email and tears immediately filled my eyes. I had failed—a 68%. SIXTY-EIGHT PERCENT. I choked back the sobs as I continued to read. Since I had failed to reach the minimum of 70% on the exam, I was given an F in the class and would be required to repay the tuition and retake the class. I couldn't speak.

I just sat there. In shock at first, then the ugly cry and then complete rage.

How could they?!! How could I?!! Looking back, it seems like such a small thing, but at the time it was a growing mountain that I was not sure I had the strength nor the skills to climb. It had felt like such a sacrifice of both time and money to do that ONE class. My first prerequisite. FAILED! I began to rethink my decision to go to graduate school. Intense doubt filled my mind, and I could almost perceive a cloud of darkness taking shape in my soul. My family was beginning to stir, and unsure how to process the news, I decided to keep it to myself for a little while.

We had a long way to drive that day, and I spent much of it looking out the window rather than playing an umpteenth game of UNO with the kids. As the afternoon approached, Dan asked me how I would feel about driving. I hesitated because I had never driven a motorhome, and even avoided driving our own truck. He hadn't slept well the night before, and after days on the road he could use a nap (well-deserved I might add). He gave me a quick lesson on how to drive the motorhome and assured me that I would be "fine." He exited the next off ramp and we made the switch.

With the kids all surprisingly entertained, and Dan asleep in the back, it was just me and the road. I was cautious at first, white knuckling it for the first hour, but soon got the hang of it. Simple. Just like riding a bicycle. After a few hours, Dan awoke, climbed into the passenger seat and offered to drive. I was feeling pretty proud of myself and told him that I was good but that we needed to get gas. We exited the freeway and found the nearest gas station.

As I turned into the gas station, I heard a terrible noise. An awful scraping sound that I couldn't pinpoint. A sound of metal on metal, but I had no idea where it came from. I pulled up beside the gas pump, and when I jumped out of the driver's seat, I was surprised to see an officer approaching me. He looked back over his shoulder at the large gas station sign on the side of the road and then to the side of the motor home. My eyes followed his gaze to a huge gash along the entire side of the rented vehicle (which was brand new and the first time the owner had decided to rent it out...UGH!). It took me a second to comprehend what had happened, but as soon as it registered in my brain, I completely lost it. Totally and completely. I began sobbing uncontrollably. Dan was just barely coming around his side of the motorhome when I collapsed in his arms. He and the officer shared glances (one of those I'm-not-really-sure-what-is-going-on-with-her-but-there's-no-way-I'm-going-to-utter-a-word kind of looks), and I just wept and blubbered about not being able to drive trucks...or motorhomes...and that he shouldn't have let me drive....because I couldn't do anything...not anything. And then in a really ugly cry, I ashamedly confessed that I had wasted our money and that I had FAILED organic chemistry.

Now I've known for a long time that I had married a very patient man, and in this instance, he became a saint. He took me in his arms and gently eased me into the passenger seat. He worked out things with the officer and the store owner while I hung my head and sobbed. My poor kids sat in silence while I tried to pull myself together. Definitely not my best moment.

It had been a long day, and that night we decided to pull off the freeway and just park on a small country road in Wyoming. We all slept soundly, and when I awoke at the crack of dawn, I felt an overwhelming sadness. I opted to not go for my morning run, and to embrace the sadness instead. I laid there only for a moment before I heard a voice in my head. This voice is hard to describe because it SOUNDS like my own voice, but it FEELS like it comes from a far-off place. A higher place, and a higher power. It has taken time, but through special rare and sacred occasions, I have learned to know this voice.

"How long are you going to cry? It's a failed test and it's a damaged motorhome. This isn't 'hard.' Look out the window. Look around you. You are in a special place where pioneers have forged their way west. What they endured was hard.

"Retake the test, Charity. Get the motorhome fixed. Wipe your tears and get out of bed. You are stronger than you think. Hard things are coming your way and I need you ready."

I did get the motorhome fixed, and the owner was unbelievably gracious (as was Dan who took on most of that burden). I also retook Organic Chemistry—this time at a different school—and I got an A.

However, my hardest lesson in resilience was yet to come.

PRACTICAL TOOLS to build Resilience:

1. **Set the Expectation.** Believing is the first step. Having the confidence in your abilities and the belief that you will bounce back is critical in developing resilience. This may be a place for personal affirmations. They might sound a little cheesy to some, but a constant reminder that you are stronger than you think

you are can have an immense impact on your beliefs.

2. **Find the silver lining.** Research has found that the emotions of people who are highly resilient are remarkably different from those who are not. The key is positivity. Both resilient and non-resilient people acknowledge and feel negative emotion, but a resilient person will simultaneously try to find a positive emotion. This can be achieved by challenging our reactive thoughts and improving our self-talk. It's back to the simple lesson from the Little Engine that Could ... "I think I can, I think I can." Be optimistic!

3. **Transform the Pain.** When we experience difficult challenges in life, we can look at them as an opportunity to grow. What can I learn from this experience? Who will I be able to help by overcoming this hardship? By seeking for solutions rather than sorrow, by aiming to overcome rather than be overwhelmed, we can transform our trials into triumphs.

4. **Practice Self Care.** Taking care of yourself with healthy habits is a foundational piece of mental and emotional resiliency (we'll learn more with Skill #6). Exercising, eating right, and getting enough sleep will give you the strength you need to get through some of the

harder times. Daily habits have a tremendous impact on building resilience

5. **Don't forget to laugh.** Life is meant to be enjoyed and not merely endured. Find a sense of humor despite the hardship. Laughing can help you stay committed to your life and your goals. Dan can find amusement in almost any situation, and because of it he has brought laughter instead of tears into our home many times.

CHAPTER 3

HARNESS HOPE

"We must accept finite disappointment, but never lose infinite hope"

- Martin Luther King, Jr.

Let's be honest, this life can be tough sometimes. If you're young enough, and this hasn't been your experience, then good for you! Keep shining, keep smiling, and be a light to others. But, if you've been around for a bit, you've likely seen some of the hard stuff that life can throw at you. Financial difficulty, betrayal, abuse, addiction, infidelity, suicide, illness, infertility, disappointment, heartache, loneliness ... I could go on but I was starting to depress MYSELF!

There's an old saying that "there are only two things you can be certain of in this life: death and taxes." Well, I might add a third: plain old hard things. And sometimes those hard things, when you're in the midst of the fire, can seem heavier than even death and taxes!

Which bring us to the 3rd skill—the ability to harness hope. The art of being able to find the silver lining in any situation. The belief that the best is yet to come. The aptitude to sing out, like that popular little red-headed orphan, that the sun will come out tomorrow! If resilience is the skill that will put the furrow in your brow as you put your shoulder to the wheel, then hope is what can put a glimmer in your eye and a smile on your face as you push along.

Hope is an interesting concept and it can evoke different emotion from different people. But for me, hope is an acquired skill, or a gift perhaps, that can change a life more than almost anything else. I believe it's a skill that can be learned, or rather earned. And it takes dedication and diligence.

Hard times are inevitable. I used to buy into the idea, "Oh it's only hard if you think it's hard … just change your perspective." But as much as I can appreciate rose-colored glasses, some things in life are just hard. Some situations just suck. A sick child, a flat tire, a failed company. I don't care how you spin it, to me these things just bite. But what I have learned is that while perspective is certainly powerful, there's nothing quite as amazing as hope. The belief that better days are still ahead. The thoughts that not every day will be like today. The assurance that the world is still good and that things can still get better. When you feel like you are drowning, hope can be the very breath that can save you.

Channeling Hope

On August 17, 2015 our lives changed forever.

Dan had been experiencing some stomach problems and bowel issues. He's pretty private about these sorts of things (his dad is British and quite proper after all), but after what he would later confess was about a year, he finally went to see the doctor. A colonoscopy was scheduled, and during the routine procedure, the technician sadly told him that she couldn't finish the exam—a tumor was blocking his colon.

I can't even imagine what went through his mind that afternoon coming home from the clinic. I'll never forget the look in his eyes when he asked me to come into our master bathroom, away from the children, away from the house full of my family members, staying with us for a family reunion. The words were searing the moment they escaped his mouth and hit my ears and my heart. He had colon cancer. He had turned forty-three two days earlier.

The colonoscopy aggravated the tumor and an emergency surgery two days later revealed that the cancer had already spread to his lungs and to his liver. My eyes fill with tears even as I type these words. Nothing can quite prepare you for those words, and you hope that you've built up enough resilience in your life to help you get through. Shock hits immediately, then grief, pain, and fear all battle for dominance in your heart and mind. If anyone has ever

63

gone through any such experience, just know that my heart aches with you.

That week was a blur, trying to manage the hospital stay and grasping for an understanding of what it all meant. We met with an oncologist, and quickly learned that there was no "hope." They suggested chemotherapy beginning immediately and thought that he had twelve months left, eighteen if all went well. The diagnosis was terminal but chemotherapy could possibly slow the growth.

Now I hesitate to share my story. Because cancer is a beast, and everyone that has ever, or will ever, go through it will navigate it in their own unique way. I have no judgment on anyone's decision. I have eaten humble pie so many times, and the things I thought I knew have all been challenged. And so I pause, to just offer love, and to simply share our experience.

For me, the idea of no hope was unacceptable. It wasn't congruent with my beliefs of the universe or the things that I had been studying for years. I had previously read, and continued to read, of miraculous stories of healing and radical remissions. I believed in so many incredible elements of healing. I believed love could heal. Laughter could heal. Herbs could heal. Prayers could heal. Friendships, medicines, kindness, nature, hope—I believed they could all heal. And that belief carried me those first few months.

This time it was my turn to share my vision with my husband and I HOPED for something more than the doctors were offering us.

In the time preceding Dan's diagnosis, I had spent countless days, months, and years studying cancer. There was no real reason for it, and I couldn't explain my draw. Seven years previous, I had inexplicably developed a passion for all things health and wellness, particularly cancer. My nightstand was constantly overflowing with books about nutrition and disease. During that time, I had become certified as a nutritionist, started a business, and had small cooking segments on the local news. I was teaching "Cancer Prevention Through Nutrition" cooking classes throughout the valley and had been accepted to graduate school to study nutrition science. When teaching my classes, people would often ask what got me started. My honest response was always the same, "I can't describe it, there's just something in my soul".

And so our battle to fight cancer began. I use the word "our" because that has what it has been from day one. God had brought us together "and the two shall become one flesh; so they are no longer two, but one flesh." Dan fought on the front line and I did my best to command the troops. Dan was, and still is, a little more in the "conservative" camp, and I tended to lean a little more to the alternative side. But I knew that our best shot was facing cancer together.

We decided to get a second opinion, and then a third. We went to multiple doctors and the outlook was always the same. "I'm sorry this is happening to you, but there's really nothing that can be done."

In my earlier research on cancer, I had heard of clinics in other countries that had had some success with alternative treatments. I began my feverish research, looking up clinics all over the world, seeking one that combined traditional and alternative methods. There were clinics in Mexico that seemed the most promising and I pleaded to God to know if that was a path that we should pursue. We went back to the oncologists to inquire about this possibility and they informed us that the doctors in Mexico were charlatans and that were preying upon our hope. Hope. Preying on my hope. I couldn't fully understand. My brain didn't really compute. What hope? It seemed there was none to be had. I was crushed and went back to the all too familiar fetal position on my closet floor. There is nothing quite as dark as no hope. Nothing.

And this thought had me wondering. If there is nothing as horrible as the path of no hope, then what's so wrong about pursuing the path that has even a little hope? I had heard of the term "false hope" in the past, and now it was time to really take a look at this enigma. What is false hope? How does it work, and who are its prey? I had been warned of this looming predator, this false hope, and yet suddenly I wanted to welcome it in and ask it to stay. False or not, it was still hope, and I begged for it.

This isn't the time or place to delve fully into our cancer journey. I'm not ready to answer cancer questions or give advice to other cancer patients. The wounds are still raw, and we are still fighting this battle every day. This book however is about skills. Tools that can change your life, and one of those, without a doubt, is hope.

We decided to take the risk and go to Mexico for treatment. Eight weeks of intense treatment in Tijuana, followed by eight weeks at home where I was required to take on the role of nurse. We did all of this for only one reason. Hope. It carried us and allowed us to dream. It gave us back our light and our laughter. The treatment was successful for a while. Until eventually the cancer came back as we had been warned. We continued with the alternative treatment for another year, and then it became evident that we needed to try something new.

At this point we both felt that it was time to start chemotherapy, and once again we found renewed hope. Ironically enough, something that we had once feared was now the grounds for our new hope. We developed an appreciation for modern medicine and there is no doubt that it has given us the gift of time. With each treatment we cling to the hope that somehow, we will beat the odds. And I guess in many ways we have. I have many opinions about alternative and conservative treatments—both have played a tremendous role that we are incredibly grateful for. As I write this, my husband has been fighting for 43 months, and I believe that hope has played a huge role in that. Although his body is no longer responding to treatment, and the tumors in his liver have caused it to slowly start to fail, still we hope. We hope for miracles and we hope for healing, but we also hope for strength, for understanding, for peace, for love, and for laughter. Hope has been a lifeline in our darkest hours, and not a day goes by that we aren't grateful for the gift of life.

Look Outside Yourself

In dealing with our struggles we found that an antidote to our own pain was to recognize the pain in others and attempt to ease it. When life gets you down, and you feel stressed about the pressure of the world, it's easy to get stuck with a mirror in your hand—metaphorically speaking of course! It's easy to start to wallow, it's easy to compare everyone else's Pinterest perfect days to your rotten luck, and it's so easy to play the victim and hold on to all the reasons why YOUR hard is just SO hard. It's in these precise moments that you need to stop looking at yourself and turn your focus to lifting others. Helping others see that they still have so much to hope for helps us do the same with our own struggles. I promise, there will ALWAYS be someone else with a heavier burden that they are carrying. While there were plenty of days that our own trial felt pretty darn hard, there were also other trials that I was so glad we weren't facing. Cancer is a difficulty that is surrounded by love. People praying for us, dropping by to check on us, or simply texting us to let us know that they care. There are many other hardships that don't come with such love. Abuse, addiction, and infidelity, along with so many others, are often clouded with pain, suffering, and shame. These people are equally deserving of love and messages of hope.

So in the moments when life seems particularly hard, and even when life is smooth sailing, find ways to share the burdens of others. Find ways to offer hope to those who might need it even more than you do. When we are standing on firm ground, it is easy to reach out and lift a hand. However, when our own foundation seems to be shaking, the very healing balm our unsteady souls seek can be found in being a source of hope to others. Victoria Ruvolo is a glowing example of this. I share her story as published in the Deseret News (Aug. 21, 2005, p. AA3).

"How would you feel toward a teenager who decided to toss a 20-pound frozen turkey from a speeding car headlong into the windshield of the car you were driving? How would you feel after enduring six hours of surgery using metal plates and other hardware to piece your face together, and after learning you still face years of therapy before returning to

normal—and that you ought to feel lucky you didn't die or suffer permanent brain damage?

"And how would you feel after learning that your assailant and his buddies had the turkey in the first place because they had stolen a credit card and gone on a senseless shopping spree, just for kicks?

"This is the kind of hideous crime that propels politicians to office on promises of getting tough on crime. It's the kind of thing that prompts legislators to climb all over each other in a struggle to be the first to introduce a bill that would add enhanced penalties for the use of frozen fowl in the commission of a crime.

"The New York Times quoted the district attorney as saying this is the sort of crime for which victims feel no punishment is harsh enough. 'Death doesn't even satisfy them,' he said.

"Which is what makes what really happened so unusual. The victim, Victoria Ruvolo, a 44-year-old former manager of a collection's agency, was more interested in salvaging the life of her 19-year-old assailant, Ryan Cushing, than in exacting any sort of revenge. She pestered prosecutors for information about him, his life, how he was raised, etc. Then she insisted on offering him a plea deal. Cushing could serve six months in the county jail and be on probation for 5 years if he pleaded guilty to second-degree assault.

"Had he been convicted of first-degree assault—the charge most fitting for the crime—he could have served 25 years in

prison, finally thrown back into society as a middle-aged man with no skills or prospects.

"But this is only half the story. The rest of it, what happened the day this all played out in court, is the truly remarkable part.

"According to an account in the New York Post, Cushing carefully and tentatively made his way to where Ruvolo sat in the courtroom and tearfully whispered an apology. 'I'm so sorry for what I did to you.'

"Ruvolo then stood, and the victim and her assailant embraced, weeping. She stroked his head and patted his back as he sobbed, and witnesses, including a Times reporter, heard her say, 'It's OK. I just want you to make your life the best it can be.' According to accounts, hardened prosecutors, and even reporters, were choking back tears".

In what was likely some of her greatest suffering, instead of focusing on her own ordeal, Victoria was able to see the need of others. She wasn't blinded by rage, or consumed with her own struggles, and no one would likely have blamed her if she were. Rather, she had the ability to look outside herself and offer love and hope to the very person doing her harm. This story is about forgiveness but it's also about the lives that can be changed when we can turn outward to be a source of hope to others.

A Lost Car

There are some things I'm good at and there are some things that I'm embarrassingly bad at. I'm quite geographically challenged. OK, and directionally challenged, but luckily Google Maps allows me to hide that one. But I'm also terribly unobservant. Almost comically unobservant. Dan used to bring home a different car each night when he worked at Enterprise Rent-A-Car. I would then drive that same car to the gym in the morning before he left to work. I can't even count how many times I would come out of the gym and have NO IDEA where my car was. Not just where is was parked, but the make, model or even color of the car. Keyless remotes were MADE for people like me.

These, let's just call them characteristics, came to a head when I decided to take a girl's trip to Portland for a weekend with two of my sisters-in-law. I love seeing new cities, and we picked Portland for precisely that reason. We rented a car, and I was the designated driver. As we were exploring the city, I reminded the girls that I would likely need a little help remembering where I parked the car (and what color it was)!

On our last morning there, we had a couple of hours before we needed to head to the airport. We went downtown for a bite to eat and some last-minute shopping. The weather wasn't great, and when it started pouring rain, we decided to go to the airport early. As we made our way back to the car we quickly realized that we didn't remember where we had parked. We had a rough idea what street the car was on, so we headed in that direction. As I'm sure you've guessed by now, the car wasn't there. We were certain it was on that street, or at least somewhere close. We hadn't walked too far, after all.

We searched one street over. And then the street over from there. Puzzled, we thought that there was no way we had missed and backtracked all three streets again. Still no car. We decided to split up and each take a different side street search. Once again, no car. And yes, we had the remote and pushed the button the ENTIRE time we were looking. At this point we were getting a little nervous about the time. We weren't sure what to do so we called the rental company to see if they by chance had a GPS tracking on the car. There wasn't, but we at least got the license plate number. Just then, two officers on bicycles rode by and we asked them if there was any way to find a lost car or towed car. We were worried that our parking had expired by this point and that the car had possibly been towed. The officers called a couple of tow companies, but again no luck.

By this point we were really nervous, and a little emotional. Sure, it wasn't a life and death situation, but it was incredibly stressful for all of us and tensions were high. I said a prayer in my heart, and just then the thought came to me to call American Express! I had used my card in the parking Kiosk on the street where we parked and maybe they could help. I quickly dialed the number, and they were able to easily identify the charge. Unfortunately, all they could give me was the address to the parking company that handled the billing. Our map showed that it was only half a mile away, so in the pouring rain we ran as fast as we could to Portland's City Parking Office. Luckily, they were able to go through the electronic receipts and write down the coordinates of the parking meter where I had swiped my credit card. As soon as we read the address we immediately looked at each other. We had been on that street. We had scoured both sides, up and down. Not once, not twice, but at least three or four times. We had walked along that entire street, while at the same time pressing the buttons on the keyless remote. We didn't see the car once. We hurried out of the office, ran to the street, and sure enough, there was the rental car.

As we were driving to the airport, I was so frustrated. How could I have forgotten where we had parked? And how could we have not seen the car in all of our searching? It just didn't make sense. Right then I had a very distinct impression. The feeling I got was that somehow, we had been protected. For some reason that I will likely never know, we were simply not supposed to get in our car before that moment. I again had the sense that we had been protected and suddenly my perspective changed. My feelings quickly

74

changed from feelings of frustration to those of gratitude.

Hope is a little like this story. Hope gives perspective to just about any situation. Like the north star, if you can keep it in sight, hope will always point you in the right direction.

But What If It's You

Up until this point we've been talking about finding hope in a world that can unexpectedly (and even expectedly) throw challenges your way. But what about when YOU are the challenge in someone else's world? What if YOU'RE the HARD? What if you're the instigator, the betrayer or the one that has done the harm? Where is the hope then? What if the shame of what you have done is so terrible that there can't possibly be anything bright in your future?

To you ... ESPECIALLY to you ... I say that there is ALWAYS hope! There is no sin so dreadful, no wrong so horrific, no wound so deep, that heaven can't reach you. If changes are needed in your life, then read on to the next chapter and embrace those changes. If forgiveness is needed, then ask for the forgiveness and then put your hope in people. Hope that hearts can be healed. Hope that wounds can be bound. Hope that things WILL NOT always be exactly as they are right now. Don't ever lose hope - even in yourself!

Overcoming Fear

By this point we have addressed three of the seven skills; having the vision to see your path, the resiliency to overcome hardships, and the hope for a brilliant future. With these in mind, it's time to address one of life's greatest hurdles, and something that will try to undermine these skills: FEAR!

Fear is your most crippling opponent and if you are not watchful, it can steal your life, your light, and your joy. In today's age the media is replete with messages of fear and despair. We are being bombarded on all fronts with reports of the most distressing nature. Natural disasters, wars, terrorism, crimes against humanity, financial collapse, predators of our children, toxins in our food supply, global disruptions of every variety … the list is long and daunting. It feels that in today's world there is no shortage of things to fear.

But you were not meant to live a life of fear!

Resilience and hope combine to create incredibly powerful weapons that can penetrate even the greatest of fears. Resiliency is the belief that there is nothing that you can't overcome and hope gives you the courage to be able to endure ALL things.

So your job is to challenge fear on all levels. Yes, it's true that fear can be a powerful motivator over our behaviors and our actions. It's probably the only reason I wear a seat belt! But fear rarely has the power to move us forward or to transform us into who we REALLY want to be. Fear can create action, but fear can never create the *feelings* in us that are necessary to sustain long-term growth. Fear stifles the feelings that keep us invigorated and motivated to keep going. Fear brings with it emotions that can leave us feeling anxious, resentful, defiant, or angry, and these emotions will not bring the life that you are seeking.

So often fear can grip us and leave us stammering and unable to push forward. A simple thought can sometimes be enough to unravel us. Your loved one is late getting home, the weather is bad, and suddenly thoughts of the worst kind come flooding. These "imaginary" fears can be immobilizing. Even worse are the real-life situations that cultivate genuine worry and fear. A lost job and the fear of paying the bills. The loss of a loved one and the fear of being alone. A health diagnosis that leaves us with the fear of losing our lives. Trust me, I know these fears. I have tasted the bitterness of true fear, and I know how debilitating it can be. But I have also found ways to overthrow fear, and one of those ways in what I call the "what-if game". Don't let the word "game" minimize the power of this potent strategy.

The "what if game" involves mentally connecting our thoughts all the way to the end of a scenario. Oftentimes, when we have a fearful thought, we allow that initial thought to become the basis of our fear.

But what if we continued that thought with another thought, ideally one that offered a solution or a blueprint to navigate through the fear. What if I lost my job? Then maybe I'd have to sell my house. But where would we live? I would have to move in with friends or family. And what if I had to that? ... you just keep playing the what if game. But take it all the way through. All the way to the very end of your greatest fears. Like draining a hot air balloon, being able to conceptualize a plan of action to even the biggest challenges is a powerful tool that can take the air out of our fears. One of my favorite quotes says, "Everything will be right in the end. If it's not right, it's likely not the end." You have the power to calm your fears. You have the power to believe that there is nothing you can't handle! Your future is as bright as your hope!

One of my greatest fears was losing my husband. It was a silent fear that I've had my whole life and one that instigated my determination to get my degree before starting a family. "Just in case anything ever happened" is what I would say (even before getting married). Well that something happened. Short of having someone abuse my children, the threat of losing my husband was as awful as anything I could imagine. And it happened. Terminal cancer.

In the beginning we were forced to play the "what if game" all the way through. What if it was cancer? Then we would fight it with everything we knew.

What if it wasn't enough? Then we would make the best of every minute. What if those minutes were taken? Then what?

While these are thoughts that I rarely dwell on, I did have to go through the best- and worst-case scenarios in my mind. I had to play it all the way out. I had to face fear squarely in the eyes. With tears brimming but shoulders squared, I took the what ifs all the way to the end.

And here is what I discovered: everything is going to be okay. I tremble even writing it. But it's the truth. As painful as it has been, as much as I wish it would all just go away, me, Dan, the kids, we are all going to be okay. No matter what. I know that even in the worst possible scenario, as much as I beg and plead to not have to face it, I know that we will come out victors. Fear will not overpower us. And as much as I fear that my happiness will be gone forever, I have tearfully vowed that even then ... EVEN THEN ... fear will not take our joy and fear will never steal our love.

Dan and I would both acknowledge that we are so much stronger today than we were 3 years ago. The hard is still hard. Cancer is still cancer. But we now have strength to get through the struggles. And not to just squeeze through, but to come out better. Kinder. More compassionate. More aware of life. And how we want to live it. So we choose, love, hope, and joy.

Our journey may be unique to us, but the principle of hope applies to everyone. No matter the misfortune, never give up. No matter how deep the wounds, however long they last, whatever the source, or whenever they happen, NEVER GIVE UP! Don't get discouraged. Things have a way of working out. Don't dwell on the problems. Be happy. Be believing. And remember that fear is one of the greatest thieves of hope! Fight for the love, the laughter, the peace, and the wisdom that this life has to offer. There is nothing that you can't get through. Nothing. So often our greatest struggles become our biggest teachers. Hope will carry you through.

PRACTICAL TOOLS to Harness Hope:

1. **Recognize that no hardship lasts forever.** If you want a sure way to stay totally miserable forever, convince yourself that things will never change and that they will always be exactly as they are. Luckily, enough life experience will teach you that this simply isn't the case. The clouds do part, the sun does come out.

2. **Smile..for the love...PLEASE smile.** There's a great phrase, "fake it 'til you make it" and this works perfectly with smiling. In fact, studies now show that when you smile, your brain actually releases dopamine and serotonin. This means that a simple smile can trick your brain into feeling happier. And the best part is, that when I see other people smile, it seems to trick MY brain too... because I always leave feeling a little happier myself.

3. **Find gratitude in the trial.** This might be one of the hardest things to actually do and I don't suggest it lightly. But I have personally found that in my darkest hour, when I can find something...anything...positive about the hardship, it helps tremendously. There are lessons to be learned everywhere, so look for the lessons and find gratitude in those.

4. **Avoid too much rumination.** The word "ruminate" comes from the Latin meaning for chewing cud, a process in which cattle grind up, swallow, then regurgitate and rechew their feed. Hear me out on this. Ruminating means that you are constantly thinking about the various aspects of situations that are upsetting to you. It involves overthinking, analyzing an issue at length, and possibly even wallowing. These actions can reinforce a depressive rut because negative outlooks hinder our problem-

solving abilities. Stop your brain from looping and leave the ruminating for the cows!

5. **Find ways to lift and support others.** Sure, it's nice when we receive love and support, but research shows that you get a greater mood boost from providing support to others. So find ways—both great and small—to help others: send a card, be a listening ear for a friend, volunteer, do something nice for somebody.

CHAPTER 4

COMMIT TO CONNECTING

"Our journey isn't meant to be an inward journey alone, but an outward journey of connection as well. When we go inward, and our heart is open, we will connect with the heart, and the heart will compel us to go outward and connect with others."

— James Doty, Into the Magic Shop

My father (also named Dan) was raised by his Irish-Catholic grandmother and his single mother, my Nona. His dad (my grandfather) had a rough go after fighting in the war. He was part of a bomber squadron and he operated the radio that kept the crew in touch with the other bombers and the airbase. His positioning in the plane was a dangerous one that left him vulnerable to enemy fire. His best friend would often ask to switch places in the plane, but my grandfather would decline, saying it was too dangerous. On the one mission that he finally agreed, his best friend was killed. His name was Dan; my father's namesake. After the war my grandfather turned to alcohol to cope. He left his wife, his daughter, and my six-week old father. I never met him.

My dad grew up in Calgary, Canada, and after his second year of university he decided to take time off to travel the world. He is a philosophical man and was in search of a deeper meaning to life. His travels took him all over the world, from Turkey, to France, and eventually to India.

My mother was born in Heidelberg, Germany, where she lived a happy life with six siblings and her parents. When my mother was 14, her mother unexpectedly developed a rare infection and was taken to the hospital. She died two days later. My mother was put into foster care and the family she once knew was never the same. After finishing high school and a year of art school she too found herself traveling in India.

When my father got his first glimpse of the beautiful blonde hippie walking down the streets of Goa, his heart told him that this was what he had come searching for. They were inseparable and scrounged to save enough money for two one-way plane tickets to Canada where they were married two months later.

You might wonder why I would tell you this story, and there's really only one reason: connection—the third skill that I truly believe will help to make your life great!

I want to feel connected to you and the easiest way for me to do that is to share a little of my life with you. It's obviously a little different in a book, but if we were talking face to face and I had just shared my parent's story with you, I would now feel closer to you. I would then likely continue the conversation with questions about your own background or upbringing.

As humans we are naturally wired for connection. Our core desires are to experience love and belonging. To feel the warmth of home and the comfort of family. To be understood and accepted. To be loved unconditionally and to feel like we belong.

Information connects us (especially women). When we share intimate parts of our life with someone else, we feel more connected. When we receive these treasures that we have been entrusted with, there is an unspoken, but deeply felt bond that can unite us. Sharing our experiences helps us find commonality, and with that a common purpose.

Happiness is the common goal for all people. We simply want to be happy, and we are always in search of where the secrets of happiness lie. The assumption used to be that money brings happiness, and that's true, but only to a certain degree. Research by the Nobel laureate psychologist Daniel Kahneman showed that money only increases happiness until about $75,000 annually and after that our emotional well-being doesn't increase with income. Success is also not the golden ticket to happiness. Ed Diener researched those on the Forbes list of most successful Americans and found that 37% of them were actually

LESS happy than the average American. The question of what brings happiness has been agonized over for centuries, and what experts have concluded is this: a feeling of connection! Research shows that people who are more socially connected to family, friends, and community, are happier, healthier, and live longer than those who are less well connected. This is why it is essential to learn the skill of connection—it could change your life!

Our Nature

Charles Darwin is often associated with the term "survival of the fittest" but further inspection of his writings shows that he was much more focused on the "survival of the kindest." In fact, he argued that "communities, which included the greatest number of the most sympathetic members, would flourish best, and rear the greatest number of offspring."

While conversation may come more naturally to some than others, compassion is part of our instinctual nature. In some ways this chapter should be disqualified as a skill, since compassion is a part of our genetic makeup. Our brains are actually wired to receive pleasure and our reward centers are triggered both when we give and receive nurture from others (it's called the supramarginal gyrus and is a part of the cerebral cortex). Compassion is defined as the emotional response when perceiving suffering and involves an authentic desire to help. But here's the kicker. It takes the *perception* of suffering before a response can occur. We actually have to notice and perceive that something is off before our brains will kick in to offer help. This is where commitment to relationships comes in. Without regular connections we would never see what needs to be seen and we would become oblivious to any and all suffering, thus losing the very compassion that is our divine nature.

Use Questions to Connect

Connecting with others can be a LEARNED SKILL, and the easiest place to start is with questions. Where did your parents meet? What were you like in high school? Did you always want to be a (fill in the blank) when you grew up or did something set you on that path? People love talking about themselves (most people do), and if you've met someone that doesn't, chances are that you haven't found the right question. Most people will light up and become very engaged when you hit on the right subject.

I'm an extrovert (though I recharge alone) and I usually enjoy talking to people. This doesn't come naturally for everyone but learning to ask questions is a great place to start. A simple question can break the ice and begin the sometimes-awkward stage of initial connection. I remember when I was a little girl, walking into my older brother's room when something caught my eye. I noticed a notepad on his desk beside his phone (remember those things that were attached to the wall with a long cord?). It had a list of questions and at the top it said, "things to ask Laura when we talk on the phone." I giggled when I read it and still smile when I think of that list. It showed his commitment to connection, and it's something simple that anyone can do.

Some people seem to be born with the gift of connection. Kari is the sister-in-law of one of my dearest friends and our paths have crossed on numerous occasions. Have you ever been around someone that just makes you feel like you are the coolest person on the planet? Kari has that gift, and when I sat back to watch how she does it, I learned a very simple (but powerful) lesson. She simply asks questions. I watched her walk right up to my teenage daughter and ask, "Now what was your name again?" "Oh that's right, and how old are you?" "What school do you go to?" "You look athletic, do you play sports?" "You're a senior, have you thought about what college you'd like to go to?" The conversation went on effortlessly. I was amazed (and taking notes). I watched my somewhat reserved daughter become relaxed and completely open up to a stranger. It was quite the sight and my mama-heart burst with appreciation for this beautiful woman who took the time to make my daughter feel worth connecting with. I sat back and watched Kari that night (and on a few other separate occasions) and she simply asks questions *with genuine interest*. Not rocket science, just commitment to caring. She has inspired me to do a little better.

Practice Listening

Perhaps even more important than speaking is learning the art of listening. It can help build solid relationships and is the foundation of strong connections. Nothing is worse than those awkward one-sided conversations, where you find yourself looking for an exit strategy. I'm sure you've all been there ... where you are trying to be inconspicuous as you frantically motion with your eyes to your friend over in the corner to come and save you! Conversations should be like a tennis match. The ball goes back and forth without spending too much time on either side of the court. This is a very simple principle, yet I am surprised by how often it is not implemented. I have been in NUMEROUS conversations where the only thing I did was smile, nod, and say "uh huh." Not one real word spoken because the person I was speaking with didn't even pause long enough to take a breath. Please don't be that person. The person that speaks on and on about whatever topic is of interest to them, with no regard for the other person. The sad thing is that they likely have NO idea! Don't be that person. Learning to listen is key to committing to connecting. I'm a naturally chatty person and it seems like I always have a story that I'm just *dying* to share, but I've learned to listen, and I've listened to learn (I'm still a work in progress).

There are a few things that can help in this area. The first is listening with the intent of understanding. And do it in a way that gives people time. People often need a little time to gather their thoughts and clarify their message. Give them some time both before as well as after they say something. I've been guilty of jumping in before they have fully finished what they wanted to say (sorry kids). And on that note, *pay attention*! It is the worst feeling to be talking to someone and then to see them checking their phones, looking out the window, or to see any other body language that clearly indicates they are not interested. Eye contact, a gentle smile, or even a touch on the arm are all ways to hold a connection. And put down the phone! Finally, don't be afraid to ask clarifying questions or to restate what they said as a way to reinforce understanding and to show your interest in the conversation.

Digital Distractions

We live in a time when technology can easily create diversions that can cause the neglect of some of our most important connections. There is a very addictive nature to online video games, pornography, social media, and even the binge-watching of Netflix. The dangers that lie therein cannot be overstated. Anything that is designed to replicate reality can be cause for concern. These distractions can cause us to gradually disconnect from relationships in lieu of a more seductive counterfeit (one that often takes very little effort on our part).

Sometimes the danger is in the device but more often it is in the missed opportunity of time that could have been used to develop or improve more important relationships. One of the greatest things we can do is to show up for people. To sacrifice our own time in order to be there for someone else. Distractions of all sort can steal that precious time. Time that could have been spent talking, laughing (or crying) together, and building long-lasting bonds with emotional currency. Sometimes the seemingly innocent nature of our digital devices disguises them from being seen as the very demise of our interpersonal skills and emotional intimacy. Check in with yourself and evaluate if this is an area that is becoming a problem. Sometimes the only way to really know is to give it up for a week or two—whatever "it" may be. Studies have found that people report an increase in overall happiness after going just seven days off social media.

Be Interested ... even if you're pretending!

I hate baseball.

It's long, it's boring, and I sometimes like to get a rise out of my husband when I tell him that baseball players aren't really even athletes. All they do is hit something with a stick. Can't a 3rd grader do that?

But there was a time that I was a fan. Or at least I pretended to be. I was in 9th grade and there was a baseball diamond just up the street from my house. Being the boy-crazy teen that I was, as soon as I found out that my latest crush had weekly games at that park, I quickly showed my interest in the sport. I would casually ride my bike to the park with some girlfriends, and spend hours in the stands, showing what dedicated fans we were. I would then attempt some casual lingering so that we "accidentally" bumped into him after the game. I remember begging my little sister (nine years younger) to walk to the park with me so we could go watch a game. The crush didn't last long, and neither did my interest in baseball (until Dan and I were dating, and he invited me to go to Denver for a Rockies game. To which I replied, "Oh, I would LOVE that!").

Here's my point. If there is someone that you would like to connect with, BECOME interested in what they are interested in. This isn't about being inauthentic or turning into a chameleon that constantly changes based on their surroundings. It's about caring enough about someone ELSE that you momentarily put aside your own interests in an attempt to understand their world just a little bit better. And doing it in a real and GENUINE way! Asking questions to sincerely learn more about their interests and not just for accolades (people can smell a fake). I am always so deeply touched when people who know a little about my life or my hobbies take the time to dig a little deeper and ask me about them.

My kids are getting older with two of the four already moved out of the house. The thought of them one day getting married has me a little petrified. If I'm being totally honest, I selfishly like my family just as it is and I'm not looking forward to changes in that area. I've seen the problems that can arise with the introduction of new family members, and quite frankly, I want to avoid that for as long as possible (sorry kids!). Now on that note, of course I want my kids to fall in love, get married, and have a family of their own (just not yet). I love my kids and I'm determined to love who they love. In order to make that process a smooth one, I've made a silent commitment to become interested in whatever they might be interested in. If I have a son-in-law who loves fishing or hunting, I will learn a little about fishing or hunting. Better yet, I'll have HIM teach me about those things by asking questions. Things like, "What's the difference between a 'good' fishing rod and a 'bad' one?" Or, "If you could choose any gun to own, what would it be?" (Clearly, I don't know much about either of those because it took me about five minutes to even come up with decent questions to ask)!

I think daughters-in-law might be a little harder to connect with. I am fiercely protective of my boys, and I'm going to have to loosen my desire to "keep them all to myself" when they decide to someday pop the question. But like I said, I'm determined to love who they love! The easiest way that I know how to do that is to show them that I'm interested in them. If she likes the ballet, then we'll get tickets to the ballet. If she wants to sell Pampered Chef then by golly I'll grit my teeth and host a Pampered Chef party for her. You see the point, right? It's one thing to tell someone you love them and it's an entirely different thing to give them the gift of your time.

Our Closest Can Be Our Hardest

I'm going to get really personal here.

I'm not super close to my parents.

I cringe even writing that because it's not something that we have ever discussed openly. We tend to keep things on the surface and maybe by the time this book is published—or maybe because it is published—I will have had the courage to talk about this with them.

I left home when I was 18, moved 36 hours away, and we've never lived within 600 miles of each other since. We haven't been very close, and clearly the distance doesn't help. It's hard to pinpoint exactly why we aren't tight, and I've had long discussions with Dan, myself (yes I talk to myself), and even God about why this is. If I were forced to narrow it down to one thing, I would say that I have never felt that my parents were really that interested in me. I played three different sports in high school. My dad was a very busy bread-winner, and my mom was juggling six kids (along with some others that she watched for extra income). This meant that they rarely, if EVER, saw my games. And it wasn't just the games. They didn't really know my friends, my classes, or my hobbies. When I moved out, I felt "out of sight out of mind." Don't get me wrong, they are great people, they love their family, and we have a nice relationship. They call, ask how the kids are, ask how Dan is, see if there's "anything new," and that's the gist of it. They'll tell me about tennis, about the latest garage sale, about their friend's son that just got married, about another friend who is moving, and so on. The whole time, I smile and do my best to ask questions and to be interested. We say our I love you's and do the same thing in a couple of weeks. They are amazing people, and everyone who knows them loves them … but we simply aren't that close.

There are two reasons that I share this story. The first is that it's likely that there are people in your life that you wish you were a little closer to. Was there a certain someone that immediately came to mind when you read my story? Are there people in your life that you know you should be a little closer to but aren't? Have you allowed any important relationships to get stale? Would those that you care about most say that they feel connected to you? The first step in fixing a relationship is to see what YOU can contribute to the relationship! Dig deep and look at YOUR actions. Can you work harder to let them know that you care? Can you make a call, send a text, mail a card ... something ... anything ... that shows that they are worth the effort?

The second reason I shared about my parents is to highlight another element of connecting. And this one is my fault entirely. In those relationships that you are TRULY COMMITTED to, you will have the courage to ASK for what you need. If you have put in the work, if you have done YOUR part in maintaining the relationship and you are STILL not getting what you need, then it's up to you to ASK. I remember as a newlywed, after a long tear-filled first fight with Dan, finally telling him what was "really" bothering me. And I remember him saying, "How in the world was I supposed to know that?! Had you simply TOLD me, it would have been the easiest thing to fix. But Babe, I can't read your mind you know!" Oh I know that... Now!!! But that took time to understand.

Sure, it would be nice if people instinctively knew just what you needed. But they don't! So it's up to you to graciously, kindly, and lovingly tell them what you need. And then to graciously, kindly, and lovingly allow them to tell you what they need from YOU! Is there a relationship that you let go sour because you weren't committed enough to ask for what you needed? And is it possible that while it dwindled you were telling yourself that THEY simply weren't filling your needs and that THEY were the ones who weren't committed. In reality, YOU may have been the uncommitted one here. Personally, I am SO guilty of being a coward in this area. I am way more likely to simply let things fade rather than work up enough courage to ask for what I need. To be TRULY committed to connecting means staying dedicated to put in the work, even if that work is hard or makes us uncomfortable. It's possible that people were willing to connect in the exact ways you needed if only they knew.

Admittedly I am a total hypocrite, because I obviously haven't had the courage to do that with my own parents. But do you want to know the even sadder truth? It's not even about courage anymore. The real truth is, that I just don't care enough to make the effort. Which is just so awful to even write. Things with them aren't "bad." Things are "fine." So why risk rocking the boat or hurting feelings when things are just fine? Well here's why. HERE IS WHY PEOPLE!!! Because that's how relationships DIE. The opposite of love isn't hate. The opposite of love is INDIFFERENCE! It's not being so mad at someone you could scream, it's simply not caring enough to put in any effort whatsoever. I'm not saying that every relationship is meant to last, and I'm not saying that there aren't toxic relationships out there that should be avoided. But what I AM saying is that our relationships are some of the most valuable things that we have in this life. And not just this life. I won't get into religion too much, but I strongly believe that our most precious relationships continue long after we leave this life. There aren't many things that last forever, so it's likely worth putting a little more effort into the things that do. And with that said, I am recommitting. Right here, right now! I am rededicated to trying harder in this area. I love my parents, and I WANT them to be in my life. So it means that I need to make a concerted effort to both fill their needs, and also communicate to them what I hope our relationship can be. Here's to fresh starts and never giving up!

Differences in How We Connect

Anyone that has been in a committed relationship for a long period of time can attest to the fact that sometimes things can feel a little "stale." This can be in a marriage, in a family, in a friendship or even in the workplace. Each one of those areas of life involve "committed" relationships. So what do you do when things just feel a little "off?" When the excitement or the energy just doesn't seem to be where it ought to be? By now you're the teacher's pet and will quickly answer that the first step is to take an inventory and look at how YOU are contributing to the relationship. What things are YOU doing to make sure that the connection stays vibrant? We all know that golden rule, "Treat others the way that you want to be treated", right? But sometimes this doesn't work. In fact, sometimes this is precisely what NOT to do!

Let me explain a lesson that took me years to fully understand.

Not everyone feels the same way I do, not everyone reacts the same way I do, and certainly not everyone feels love and connection the same way I do. So my job isn't necessarily to treat others how I want to be treated. My job is to find out how THEY want to be treated. To understand how they feel watched over, cared for and loved. Ty Bennett, noted author, speaker, and leadership trainer, calls this the Platinum Rule. "When it comes to dealing with people, communication and influence; we need to move beyond the Golden Rule to the Platinum Rule," he advises. "Treat Other People The Way They Want To Be Treated. The difference is subtle, but in practice it's drastic. It's not about you. It's about them."

Many of you are familiar with the five different love languages that were made popular by Gary Chapman: quality time, acts of service, words of affirmation, gifts, and touch. These are different ways that people feel love. I don't think this is an all-encompassing list of our individual needs, but it's a good place to start.

When I first got married, I was young and naive, and I assumed that everyone must think and feel the same way I do. I was in college at the time and remember being blown away by the principle in the book "Men are From Mars, Women are From Venus." Men and women are simply different! And this couldn't be more true with me and Dan. For years I would try to connect with him in the way that I wanted to feel connected. Which was quality time and conversation. I would want to talk and talk and talk (luckily I have girlfriends now that can save Dan from some of my needed conversations). He, on the other hand, likes to connect by doing activities together, and of course touch. Going to a basketball game and holding hands or snuggling at the movie theatre are great ways for him to feel connected. The problem was that this wasn't how I felt love. In an attempt to bring love and light into our marriage, and with very good intention, we would spend time and effort trying to SHOW love in the same way that we wanted to RECEIVE love. The problem was that neither one of us was receiving love that way.

It wasn't until we were able to recognize that we each felt connected in different ways that we were able to start GIVING love in those ways. After 23 years of marriage it still requires attention and effort. I still don't feel particularly close to him when we go to an over-crowded sporting event, but I DO feel connected knowing that my being there let's him know that I'm committed to US.

While we are on the topic of the differences in how we connect, it's imperative that we also acknowledge the differences between introverts and extroverts.

Since I am not an introvert, I was curious to see if they need connections in the same way that I do. In my research on this topic I came across an incredible book by Susan Cain called "Quiet: The Power of Introverts in a World That Can't Stop Talking." I can't say enough good things about this book! In her book, Cain describes those that prefer listening over talking, reading over partying and quiet harmony over confrontation. She describes a whole array of introverted "tendencies" rather than an all-encompassing checklist deeming one either an introvert or not. She highlights many of the differences between extroverts and introverts, and counsels, "Respect your loved ones' need for socializing, and your own for solitude (and vice versa if you're an extrovert)." She confirms my suspicion that even introverts need connection. They just do it differently. They prefer quality over quantity. Introverts tend to devote their social energies to close friends, colleagues, and family. They typically prefer one-on-one discussions over group activities. They seek deep over surface. The solid conclusion is this— regardless of where you fall on the introvert/extrovert spectrum, we all have one thing in common: connected relationships make us happier.

Connecting In The Workplace

The principles of connection are equally important in the workplace, maybe even more so. When asked what they loved most about their jobs a majority of people said, "the people I work with." When asked what they liked least, they responded "the people I work with." The greatest leaders in a company are the ones who recognize that people are worth investing in. There is a very distinct difference between the roles of a leader and a manager. Management is much more focused on being task-oriented and using metrics for measuring success. Leaders, on the other hand, are much more concerned with growth and tapping into potential. They know that growth involves change, and that relationships built on true connection can be the instrument to drive that change. Regardless of positions in the workplace, the skill of connection can be applied to the person on the other side of the cubicle just as easily as it can to a leadership position. People want to feel acknowledged, seen, understood, and ideally, they want to feel appreciated.

This same idea can be expanded when working with customers. There are multiple reasons why a customer will purchase from one retailer over another, but one of the biggest reasons is that they feel a "connection" of some sort with that company. Do you know of anyone that is completely loyal to a brand? Anytime I see someone with a Coca-Cola T-shirt on, or a baseball hat with their favorite team on it, I am reminded that these companies have made a connection. Tesla is another one that seems to have a growing fan club.

The job of a successful sales team is to figure out how to make and then improve that connection. The secret lies in understanding the needs of the customer. A sales team might THINK they are doing their best to make the connections and manage relationships, but it's possible that they are doing it in a way that doesn't resonate with the customer. This is precisely what happened with a friend of mine.

Her team worked incredibly hard and felt that they were being effective through regular phone calls and emails to their clients. They logged the days and times and showed her "how hard" they were working to stay connected. Unfortunately, this is not how her clients saw things. When my friend took time to investigate the situation, she found that phone calls and emails were not at all how her clients wanted to be approached. In fact, it was precisely what they didn't want. Her clients were physicians, and with early mornings and long days at the hospital, they didn't have time for a phone call. The emails felt tedious and rather impersonal. What my friend discovered was that a quick text checking in and making sure that they had everything that they needed was all that was required. In fact, many of the physicians later praised her for being so assertive and "in tune" with their needs. Her team thought that they had been going the extra mile, but in reality, they weren't filling the real needs of their customers. Additionally, her team likely would have avoided this disconnect had they understood the importance of asking questions and being a good listener.

Another area where the workplace is enhanced by connecting is in creating a sense of "community" which can be just as important within a company as it is in a neighborhood. This sense of community brings trust and the more we trust that the people on our left and the people on our right have our backs, the better equipped we are to face the challenges at hand. When we've reached this level of connection, it's easy to recognize because we can feel it. It might not be measurable or tangible per se, but we can still feel it. We feel cared for by our colleagues and we feel valued by our superiors. One of our most fundamental needs is being met; the need to belong.

There is a sense of safety that is established when we feel like we belong and all of the energy that was once used to try and fill that need can now be used elsewhere. People can now focus their efforts on collaboration, cooperation, and innovation. Regardless of our personality, our job title or our skill set, every single person wants to feel valued. So whether you are the head honcho or the lowest on the pecking order, a true leader understands the responsibility to make others feel valuable. To put in the effort to discover what makes them feel valued, and then to unconditionally make that offering. This is the purest form of connection, and this is what builds strong businesses, strong relationships, and strong communities.

Think Outside The Box

Keep in mind that connection doesn't always need to be verbal. Sometimes it's the little things that can make the biggest difference. Dan's first job out of college was for Enterprise-Rent-A-Car and he was putting in long hours, six days a week. With three small children at the time I was feeling burned out. As a reward for his hard work, Enterprise was flying Dan to Florida for what appeared to me to be a four-day party. I was becoming a little resentful of his business lunches, his golfing with clients, and now his trip away. Truthfully, I was feeling underappreciated and was jealous of the validation he received at work, and jealous of his all-expense-paid "work" trip.

Then something interesting happened. The night before his trip there was a knock on the door and a small gift basket left on the porch. When we looked at it, it was for me! There was movie popcorn, some theater treats, and a gift card to Blockbuster (anyone remember video cassettes?). The best part was a little note that said something along the lines of "thanks for sharing your husband with us. We know it's not always easy. Here's a little something to make the weekend go by more quickly." I was shocked. Full-on-jaw-to-the-floor shocked. And right then my perspective changed. I felt understood, and I felt appreciated. And all it took was a little effort and less than twenty bucks! True leaders understand that a little connection can go a very long way.

Reverse Networking

When I was about to graduate with my bachelor's degree, I remember so many professors telling us to make sure that we were "networking." I didn't really understand what they meant. Over time I came to understand the idea behind networking. It meant staying connected so that you would know when job opportunities arose. According to a recent survey and LinkedIn article, "85% of all jobs come from networking." While all this is likely true, I've observed something far more interesting in my co-founder of Silver Fern, and dear friend, Phil. He is what I call a master "reverse networker." He knows EVERYONE, and he uses that skill to simply improve people lives. He thrives off of connecting people with other people that might fill a need they have. I've watched so many people walk into the office, casually tell Phil about a project they are working on or a stumbling block that they've encountered, and inevitably Phil will give them the contact information of "a friend of his" that he is certain can help. It's a wonder to behold. Nothing is in it for him. Now you might be skeptical and say, "yeah, sure, but now these people 'owe' him." While that may be true, I can honestly say it's not Phil's intention to "get something out of it." It's just his nature and it's inspiring to be around. The underlying principle of networking is essentially somewhat "self-serving," whereas the concept of reverse networking is generous and altruistic. I have been able to observe Phil use the power of connection to enrich the lives of people in the office, our industry, and pretty anyone that crosses his path!

The Art of Watering

In relationships that suffer, sometimes the worst thing we can do is allow "absence to make the heart grow fonder." Sometimes these absences are actually what makes the heart grow colder. True connections take nourishing, and without it hurt and anger can begin to fester. Sometimes "taking a break" from a relationship, rather than improving the relationship, can actually make it grow stale. Planting a seed is a great analogy. If the soil is right, and the proper attention given, with sun and water the seed will begin to grow. If at some point the plant dies, it is NOT because the seed was bad, but rather that the nourishment was removed. We may be prone to look back and say, "Ah, proof that it didn't last, and likely was not a solid relationship," when upon inspection the problem was not with the people but with the effort provided to make it survive.

One of the greatest lessons I have ever learned is that love and connection are an ACTION and not merely a feeling. It's about DOING the little things that take time, intention, and effort. The kind words, the affectionate touch, or proactively spending time together. I call these the "love-actions". We've all heard the saying "the grass is greener on the other side," and an equally popular saying, "the grass is actually greener where you water it." This is physically true with grass and metaphorically true with people. Love is an action. Roughly half of the marriages in American end in divorce, and with less people actually getting married, the number of broken relationships is even higher. With irreconcilable differences being among the most common grounds for divorce, I can't help but think of how many people are "falling out of love." How many people have stopped watering? Stopped putting in the effort required to make something grow strong and beautiful. I imagine that for some there may have been a source of hurt that caused the "in-actions", but for the majority I imagine it began with something as simple as mindless neglect. With the hustle and bustle of everyday life, with deadlines and duties, with pressures and problems, there are a million different pulls on our time and energy. Which begs the question, "Are we giving our least to those that matter most?".

The sad thing is, that as our most important relationships starts to lose their luster, there is a natural tendency to begin to notice all the "wrongs" instead of all of the "rights." Unfortunately, once we start the criticism train, it's hard to make it stop. With one deep enough offense, suddenly we seem to see only evidence of ALL the other wrongdoings just waiting to be discovered! Quickly our vision becomes tainted, and now all we can see are the dark things. We must be fierce about what we focus on because we have a talent of always finding what we are looking for. When we feel our love fading it's a sign that we need to ACT, even if that means you "fake it til you make it." Remember that it is much easier to act your way into feeling than it is to feel your way into acting.

A New Perspective

I learned this lesson firsthand after 20 years of marriage. Dan and I have always had what I would say was a solid marriage. But like many long-term relationships, I began to take him for granted, and started to see the many things that were "wrong." I slowly stopped doing the "love-actions." I'm not sure how it began, but slight thoughts like "we are so different" would creep into my mind. These subtly expanded into thoughts like, "we don't really have that much in common." Slowly, ever so slowly, these ruminations developed into further criticisms. "I hate the way he drives," "he's so obnoxious when he yells at the TV during a game!" Soon it seemed like almost everything he did (or didn't do) was bothersome. Critique and judgment may seem harmless at first, but they have a wicked way of transforming into deep-rooted negative feelings over time. My "innocent thoughts" slowly began to be much more menacing.

Like a successful garden, a good marriage requires getting rid of the weeds before they grow too big. I'd like to think that my experience is unique, but I have watched many marriages fall apart when the weeds started to take over.

It took the painful experience of cancer to give me the perspective that I needed. I will forever be grateful for how quickly a horrible disease allowed me to see the important things in life. A man that I was deeply in love with. My best friend. A companion. Just something as simple as that was so easily overlooked. Someone to run errands with. Someone to share my troubles and triumphs with. Someone to talk to and touch. Someone to plan a future with and someone to sit beside at church. A man that adored me and our children. A man that made me laugh, provided for me, complimented me regularly, and a man that made my world just a little safer to live in. How could I have so easily overlooked these things? How could I have been so blinded to all the goodness, and all the light in my life? How could I not see that the single greatest decision I had ever made was this very man who I shared my life with? I get a little choked up thinking about how easily it can all be taken away. Life is short. We get one shot. We MUST be diligent in how we see things. We MUST be FIERCE about what we focus on. We have a tradition in our neighborhood at wedding showers to give the new bride some advice. Mine is always the same. Be fierce about what you focus on. Simply changing your perspective can determine your destiny.

Commit to Connecting ... even when it's uncomfortable

Sometimes in life, even when we want to stay committed we aren't sure how. So many of us think the positive thoughts, and want to help, but we don't necessarily take it further than that. Sometimes we perceive the need, our heart is in the right place, but we are uncomfortable with the suffering of others. We use words like "Let me know if there is anything that I can do," because they keep us far enough away from the fire. This story was sent to me a few years ago, and I have never forgotten it. I don't know the author but would love to thank her. Her story has helped me to recognize those people in my life that were willing to "get in the fire" with me, and it was a good reminder that I don't ever want to be the one "just outside the window."

Less than seventy-two hours after my husband told me he didn't believe in God anymore, and that he also wanted a divorce, I sat on a pew at church and waited for Sunday School to start. Turns out, the lesson was about marriage. I lasted just under three minutes before I picked up my bag, and carefully walked out to my car. It was a violently clear, sunny day in the tropics, my hands burning on the door's edge while the sky's breath and heartbreak boiled my tears.

A couple of minutes lost to sobbing, then a shadow, carrying a very hesitant and unsure "Hey... Kellie?" It was a woman freshly moved into the neighborhood, who only an hour before had sat astounded as I explained to her and a friend how my world had crashed in the course of a few sentences just days previously. I didn't even know her first name.

She crouched down next to my open door, in the glare of the sun and in the sauna humidity of the day, and let me cry. I bawled for a long time. She stayed for all of it. She didn't say anything. No words, just a quiet, sweating, tissue-passing witness to my grief and desolation.

I pulled myself a little bit together five minutes before Primary and my sons would be released back into the wild. I smiled soggily, disastrously, at her and shrugged. "It was just that topic," I tried to explain.

"I know," she said, shrugging herself. "I saw you leave, and didn't want you to feel alone."

She texted me that night. Her name was Kim.

I realized later that the church had held people I'd known for years, people who knew some or none of my catastrophe – friends and vipers both – but only one person came looking, and she didn't even know me. Later still I realized it wasn't because of indifference that my friends didn't come out, but because they were stalled, immobilized by doubt and indecision.

I'm afraid of the space where you suffer

Where you sit in the smoke and the burn

I can't handle the choke or the danger

Of my own foolish, inadequate words

I'll be right outside if you need me

Right outside

The thing is, when our lives are an inferno, someone being outside is useless. It's like the oft-used and absolutely stillborn "Let me know if I can do anything" — so full of potential, while also so tragically lifeless.

What can you do? What can any of us do? Maybe acknowledge that life, this moment, this cruel and carnivorous and devastating inferno is eating someone (ME! YOU!) alive. Recognize it, and maybe do something about THAT. Whatever 'that' is.

What can I bring to your fire?

Shall I sing while the roof is coming down

Can I hold you while the flames grow higher

Shall I brave the heat and come close with you now

Can I come close now?

I've had all sorts of fires in my life. I've wanted and needed different things at all sorts of times during each blaze. I'm incredibly blessed to have two friends who are trained, glorious singers, and there have been periods when I've wanted them to sing some gut-wrenching, Valkyrie inspired aria to accompany the disaster, burning out to sea. There have been moments when my deepest, most sincerest heart's wish is for someone to come to my fire hauling a Molotov cocktail or seven. And a Taser. With a fire-breathing, PMS'ing dragon to add a little extra flourish to the proceedings. One night I wanted someone to venture close, sit beside me, and watch the sparks of my old love letters dancing up to meet the stars.

So we left you to fight your own battle

And you buried your hope with your faith

'Cause you heard no song of deliverance

There on the nights that followed the wake

We never thought to go with you

Afraid to ask

Months — even years — after my marriage ended, people have approached me to say they wish they'd done things differently. I've approached people to apologize for not doing something, anything, even if it was a simple "I have no idea what to say — just I'm so sorry this has happened." I have to wonder sometimes if with so much perfection and Pinterest enthusiasm and posed Instagram photographs we fetter ourselves from doing a tiny something because it's not more... well, significant, well-prepared and amazing.

I wasn't left to fight my own battle in the car-park that day. Kim was nervous, and obviously uncomfortable, yet still settled herself straight down in the middle of the mess regardless. At that moment I had faltering faith, there was no song of deliverance as I realized that cherished covenants were busted, and hope was a charred, broken thing without wings. We know of Shadrach, Meshach, and Abednego being tossed into the furnace and being protected, unscathed. But life can savagely and enthusiastically remind us that sometimes it's the innocent, the loved ones, the ordinary are thrown into the fire, and left there.

Kim didn't offer to fix anything. She gave me no platitudes, no promises, no scriptural recourse or plans. She was Christlike, as when Christ – just minutes from raising Lazarus from death – first mourned with Mary and Martha, recognizing their world burning to ash and ruin. While Christ had the miraculous cure for Mary and Martha, we're not expected to raise anything, phoenix or otherwise. We are simply asked to mourn with those that mourn, comfort those in need of comfort (interestingly enough, which are detailed as being two entirely separate times, not a one time deal), to bear one another's burdens that they may be light. We're not asked or expected to take all the pain and flames away – just to lighten the burden, to sit together, in the burn. Please, to be there; in the ash, within the blaze, amid the life burning down.

What can I bring to your fire?

Shall I sing while the roof is coming down

Can I hold you while the flames grow higher

Shall I brave the heat and come close with you now

Can I come close now?

(The lyrics are to a song called "Come Close Now," by Christa Wells)

It takes a little time to understand the way some people feel loved. Honestly, it takes some time to figure out how YOU feel loved. Simply observing those you care about will give you clues, but don't underestimate the power in simply asking them what they need. What can you bring to the fire? This will look differently for everyone, and may require sensitivity, insight, and dedication. It may feel like a struggle at first, but like the other skills in this book, committing to connecting is worth the endeavor. We are born and we die, and what happens in between defines who we are. The only choice we have is in how we respond to each precious moment we are given. In the moments of pain, we can choose to offer comfort and share the pain, or we can choose to look away. One is worth the effort. So commit to connecting.

Practical tools to Commit to Connecting:

1. **Take time to reflect**. This week ask yourself these questions: Who should you connect with that you haven't? Who are the people in your life that need to know that you are committed to them? Are there people that YOU need connection from? Use a notebook or app on your phone as thoughts come to you and write down ways that you can connect.

2. **Make Special Events Special.** This was advice that I was given when I was a young mom and for some reason it hit me with such force that I never forgot it. Special events are the PERFECT time to show your commitment to connecting. I'm a "birthday person" and I feel like it's a great chance to make people feel special. Everyone deserves love, and everyone deserves to feel special on the day that was designed to celebrate THEM. So make the effort to celebrate special events. Graduations, promotions, holidays, or anniversaries! These are worth the effort. Life can get mundane, and it's these special events that deserve a little extra pizazz. I know of a few couples that don't celebrate birthdays or anniversaries, and that might work just fine for them, but my take is that it's way too easy to get lost in the monotony of life...so find ways to celebrate it!

3. **Show Up for People.** I remember hearing a friend say that there were two events in life that seem to matter more than most: weddings and funerals. She could name just about everyone that had come to her father's funeral and she was deeply touched. She was at one of her lowest moments, and she was shocked by just how much she was buoyed up by those who came to honor her father. When my father-in-law passed away, our family experienced the

same thing. Sadly, it was those who had also lost a parent who knew the pain involved and were often the ones to show their deepest support. So SHOW UP! The baby shower, the team lunch, or the school play. Sure, you might not WANT to go, and you probably have plenty of other things to do, but SHOW UP. Because people matter!

4. **Overcome the reluctance to reach out.** Put down the phone. Turn off the TV. Skip the movie and simply connect. Face to Face. Good old-fashioned communication (unless of course you want to use FaceTime or Skype to connect, then the device is of course acceptable :)). With a friend, a loved one, a child, a co-worker, a neighbor … the list could go on and on. Just CONNECT! We all have the gift and ability to connect. This will feel differently for different people. Music, poetry, art, or simply by offering a listening ear. There are a million ways to open our hearts and to speak to each other.

5. **Create an Opportunity**. It takes much less effort to feel left out than it does to create "inclusions." Plan a girl's night out. Invite the guys over to watch the game. Ask her on a date (no texting allowed). Organize a block party. Arrange a luncheon. One of our greatest fears is the fear of rejection. And because of this

crippling fear, we avoid any occasion where rejection is a possibility. So it's much "safer" to be the attendee rather than the host. But life is too short to play it safe. So put yourself out there! Plan something ... ANYTHING! The risk of having someone say no is far outweighed by the lasting connections that are likely the reward.

CHAPTER 5

EMBRACE CHANGE

"When we are no longer able to change a situation, we are forced to change ourselves."

- Victor Frankl

Change is never easy. We are creatures of habit and creatures of comfort, so anything that comes along to challenge those can instantly feel like a threat. Unfortunately, or fortunately for those who welcome it, change is inevitable. And the better able you are to embrace change in your world, the easier it will be to live your best life.

There are two types of change that are worth addressing. The first is the change that comes as a natural part of life and is about adapting to the change that is *happening* to you. Things often out of our control that come along to challenge our comfort. Perhaps a new boss, the loss of a job, or a death in the family. These types of changes can sometimes challenge us to the core.

The other change is the one that comes from within ourselves. The deeper parts of self that inexplicably call us to be better than we currently are. The desire to improve and to progress. It is the type of change that requires action on our part. Life is improved when we learn to embrace both types of change.

Thinking Like Mice

Many of you may be familiar with one of my favorite fables called "Who Moved the Cheese?" by Spencer Johnson. The simple story is about two mice and two "little people" living in a maze. Each morning they saunter over to Cheese Station C to get their beloved cheese. They are nourished and happy, and of course perfectly comfortable. But one day, the cheese isn't there. The two mice decide to go off in search of new cheese, but the two "little people" choose to stay put and wait for the cheese. What they don't know is that the cheese is never coming back to Cheese Station C.

In trying to build Silver Fern Brand (an ecommerce business that sells supplements and functional foods), I've had similar experiences in business, sometimes scratching my head and wondering "Who Moved the Cheese?" When we were a small start-up, we decided to use the "Influencer Model" as one of our main marketing strategies. I knew that we had some of the best products on the market, but I also knew that some education was needed in selling our products (like why spore-based probiotics are different and why that matters). We opted to seek out influencers on Social Media that could help us educate their followers on gut health. In the beginning this was a big success. But one day the cheese wasn't in Station C anymore. Instagram decided to change their algorithms and almost overnight we were scrambling through a maze, trying to find nourishment.

Luckily, we understood the nature of business and, like the mice, set off in search of new cheese, and were able to quickly readjust our strategies. Businesses, and even industries, seem to be changing at lightning warp speed, and not only is the cheese constantly moving, but sometimes the maze itself seems to be shifting mid-step.

Change is inevitable and our ability to adapt and embrace that change can give us the edge, along with peace of mind. Allowing team members to be a part of the decision-making process, sharing your vision with them, and reminding them that they have the resilience to succeed, can help employees through the transition process. Don't forget to celebrate successes along the way. Recognizing that change can be difficult and offering praise for the effort is a powerful leadership skill that can be a source of strength and unity to a team.

The Tools of Change

A few years ago Dan came to me and told me that he had been doing some research online and that he had the BEST idea! He excitedly said, "I think I'm going to build a swimming pool!" I was admittedly a little shocked, and thought to myself, "Does he even know HOW to build a swimming pool?" This was our first home and we had taken great pains to put in a yard. Long nights and weekends digging out every rock, trenching for sprinklers, installing the pipes, spreading topsoil and then finally laying grass. Since he had done most of the work, I felt like it was his decision to make if he wanted to dig half of it up (although I still wasn't convinced that he actually knew how to build a pool).

He was giddy and he was determined! He ordered our entire pool kit online (who knew there were do-it-yourself pool kits), and a few weeks later a semi-truck dropped two giant crates onto our driveway. Dan hired an excavator to dig the hole for the pool and then got to work. A lot of work! Many days of sweat and frustration, but little by little he began assembling the pool. A giant metal frame that seemed to fit into the ground perfectly, the entire plumbing system, the pool pump and heater, and a small fiberglass hot tub that sat just right over the kidney-shaped side of the pool. His work was beginning to look like a masterpiece. I was impressed!

128

The day finally came to install the large plastic pool liner. The last thing to be done before we could start filling it with water. We carefully removed the liner from the box, unfolded it, and with some help from neighbors we were able to get it into place. And that's when I noticed the problem. The big blue liner barely fit the edges, let alone down the sides and to the bottom of the eight-foot pool. The shiny blue liner was as tight as a drum. In fact, it looked an awful lot like a trampoline. I looked at Dan and could see the look of confusion on his face as he looked back and forth from the pool liner to the instruction manual. Something was definitely not right. Surely there was no way this newly installed "trampoline" was going to be our swimming pool. (The kids didn't mind—they figured it was a win either way!)

After a few days of trying to figure it out, Dan finally called the pool company. He explained the problem to them, and they quickly looked up his order form. After going through all of the parts, they said, "Nope, no problem, you've certainly got the right liner." Dan assured them that something was wrong, and that the liner simply was not fitting right. And that's when they asked him the magical question, "What's the temperature there Mr. Lighten?" When Dan explained that it was in the low 60's outside, that's when they identified the problem. "Ah, well there you have it," they explained. "Just wait until the temperature is up to about 72 degrees, and then turn on a hose with water. The extra heat and the pressure from the water is all you need to have your swimming pool." We were stunned. We waited until the air warmed up and the sun could give some stretch to the liner, and sure enough the liner fit like a glove. All it needed was a little heat and a little pressure.

This little lesson stuck with me and I wondered if the same principle could work on my kids. There was one particular time that things in the house were a little off, and I could sense that a change was needed. The kids had started slacking on their chores and had been fighting a little more than usual. Patience was short and tempers were running high. All four kids had their own phone at the time, and I got the feeling that it might be a source of some of the problems. I figured this was a good time to add a little pressure to instigate the change I was looking for. I felt like they were spending way too much time on their phones, and with a little incentive (ice cream at Leatherby's) I challenged them to delete all social media for one week. Luckily, they agreed. Okay, I may have used a little too much pressure (with a very stern face and hands on my hips) when "highly encouraging" them to participate. But they all said yes.

So the challenge began, and some complained while others touted this as the "easiest challenge" I had come up with. I'm not going to say that I noticed huge changes, but the subtle ones were the ones I was hoping for anyway. There was more family interaction, more "yeses" to family games (which would have easily been a "no" when lured by the phone), and honestly, it just felt like they were happier. A little heat and a little pressure were all that we needed to create some change in our home.

Mario Bros & Isaac Newton

There are times in life when we just feel stuck.

When I was a girl, Nintendo launched Super Mario Bros. I've never been much for video games, but there was just something about Super Mario that I loved! The game was designed as a side-scrolling platform that caused the player to move along the screen, from left to right, until they reached the end of a level. I remember one level that required figuring out how to scale a giant wall in order to make it to the next level. I would attempt this level over and over again trying to figure out how to get over that dang wall. Eventually I learned that there were tools that I could gather along the way that would help, along with secret bricks that would appear to allow me to scale the wall.

Life can be a lot like that video game.

In some ways we are all on our own platform, moving along nicely until it feels like we hit a wall. For many people, the gut reaction is to either turn around to try and avoid the wall, or at the very least, stand still so that we don't keep running into it. But these are the times in life when it's time to dig deep and scale the wall. It's the universe's way of saying "you've made it to the end of this level. It's time to move on to the next one." So often, fear will swoop in and convince you that it's way more comfortable to just stay where you are. Climbing walls can be difficult, and there's always the risk of falling. When I look back at my life at times that I felt "stuck," so often it was when it was time to move on to the next level. Sometimes these were big, new, scary chapters—choosing a degree, deciding to get married, having children, or starting a new business adventure—and sometimes they were small "walls" designed to simply keep me progressing in life.

One particular example comes to mind. My kids were all in school at the time and I had been teaching Food for Life classes for a few years (more to come on that). Truth be told, I was feeling a little "dissatisfied" with life—I couldn't really put my finger on it. When you're at that point, it's not always easy to identify. The feelings can be something like boredom, mixed with a restlessness along with growing discontentment. For me, it's hard to pinpoint right away, but it often feels like I've hit a bit of a wall. I've since learned that this is my soul telling me that it's time to add a little "heat", and it's time to take on a new challenge or learn something new.

At the time, we had purchased some land and were in the initial stages of getting ready to build a house. We had settled on a house design and were shopping around for builders. I remember having the very subtle thought "Why don't you build the house?" This was quickly dismissed, because that would be crazy. But the thought came again, "You could do this, you've got the time, and you could figure it out." Of course, this was insanity, I had zero experience, and a real estate license does not qualify anyone to be a general contractor. But the thought wouldn't go away, and truthfully, the thought itself wasn't that compelling. It was something else. There was a very subtle, yet undeniable feeling of excitement that would come every time I allowed myself to consider the idea. I was drawn to this invigorating feeling and found myself craving it almost like an addict. I finally realized that this was my "next level." I told Dan that I wanted to figure out how to build the house. I found oodles of information on the internet, along with a precise timeline outlining the order that I should do things. He was 100% on board! For the next eight months I ate, slept, and breathed all things "house-building" (yes, I have a slightly obsessive personality). I got permits, and financing, I hired subs, and even fired a few. With Dan by my side every step of the way we slowly started to build our dream home. There were days that I would jump out of bed at the crack of dawn with the excitement of a school girl. It was thrilling to stretch, and learn, and create. Of course, there were plenty of setbacks and plenty of tears (poor Dan). But overall it was one of the most exciting projects I have ever done. And not ONCE in that entire time did I ever feel bored or "stuck." In fact, I was being "filled" almost daily as I slowly accomplished the goal of building our home (which we still live in today). It made me reflect on the unhappiness that I had previously experienced and which completely disappeared when I decided to "climb the wall." I can't help but wonder if the dissatisfaction that we face in life is coming from a deeper place within us that desires change and progression.

Sir Isaac Newton was the first one to recognize this principle and classify it as a "law." Although he was referring to a law of motion, it applies perfectly to the idea of change. Newton's first law states that every object will remain at rest or in uniform motion in a straight line unless compelled to change its state by the action of an external force. In English terms that means that nothing changes if nothing changes. If you are unsatisfied with any area of your life, nothing will change without some sort of "action." As much as I love the virtue of a positive attitude, wishful thinking isn't actually a strategy. It's a great mind set, and hoping for improvement can encourage us to change. But simply "wishing" lacks the action that is needed to create change. Change can sometimes feel disruptive and often feels uncomfortable, but change can also be the catalyst for an exhilarating life. So if you are feeling like Mario in your life, stuck on the same level, look for the "tools" and "secret bricks" that you need and start climbing!"

True Self-Love

We've been hearing a lot about Self-Love over the last few years. Maybe not as much in the male sector, but most certainly in the female sector. And I'm all for being more gentle, accepting, forgiving, and kind with ourselves. This of course comes with the hope that when we have learned to offer these gifts to ourselves, we will be more free to offer them to others as wells.

That said, there are certain ABSOLUTES that just might not deserve "self-love" and acceptance but actually require change. One thing that sets us apart from all of the other creatures on the planet is the ability to self-evaluate, and then to make the needed changes. Some of these are simple. If you are prone to taking things that do not belong to you, CHANGE. If you are hot-tempered or violent, CHANGE. If you use your influence to intimidate or manipulate, CHANGE. Luckily, we have laws that protect us as a society from many of these character flaws.

There are however, other characteristics that may not be quite so self-evident but require just as much attention. If you are not kind, CHANGE. Our world does not need any more unkindness. If you tend to be negative, an eager complainer, or always seem to be offended, CHANGE. It will serve you and those around you to make the conscious decision to change. If you are the coworker no one can gets along with, if you are quick to gossip, stir the pot, or point out faults, CHANGE. As Mahatma Gandhi once said, *"Be the change you want to see in the world."* Individuals, and humanity as a whole, benefit when we have the humility to honestly evaluate ourselves and take the needed actions to change for the better.

This a sticky topic and in a world where selfishness is replacing service, I hope that self-love, being "authentic", more "honest," or even the idea of being more "vulnerable" does not ever equate to a "that's just the way that I am" or "take it or leave it" kind of attitude. I am not suggesting that self-care equates to selfishness, but I am suggesting that it can be a spectrum, with one end resolutely opposed to change. We must be careful that "self-love" doesn't become "self-justification" of being less than our best. The truest form of self-love is recognizing the need and then taking the necessary steps to ensure real and lasting happiness in life. As we already acknowledged, a part of that happiness comes from the connections we make. The most successful relationships will require a high degree of both mutual toleration as well as compromise. Real love can be a motivator for change, and not an excuse to forever stay as we are. True self-love is understanding the joy that comes from growth and continuously seeking out opportunities for self-improvement.

Put in the Effort

We tend to watch a lot of football in our house. Or rather, whenever a football game is on, our TV seems to miraculously get turned on. Luckily, unlike baseball, I really enjoy watching football. One of my favorite things to look for is the record of each team. Usually there will be something like a 10-3 or a 7-7 right beside the team's name telling me how many wins and how many losses each team has. And almost inevitably if there is an obvious underdog I will instantly start rooting for that team (unless of course it's the Raiders or Chargers). There's just something about the story of an underdog that gets me cheering every time. And I know it's not just me. Hollywood has learned how to make a lot of box office hits based on that exact premise.

I still remember seeing "The Karate Kid" in theaters as a child. We moved around a lot growing up, so I immediately related to the feeling of being "the new kid." I watched nervously as Ralph Macchio was harassed by the "cool kid" at school (and his karate coach was even worse than he was). I loved watching Mr. Myagi's unconventional teaching methods ("wax-on, wax-off") and my heart was pounding during the final scene where Daniel-son, against the odds, defeats his nemesis and claims the karate championship. Hollywood has capitalized on the story of the underdog, knowing that there is a part inside of each of us that desires to conquer the Goliath. Think of "Rocky," "Cinderella Man," "Seabiscuit." and "Million Dollar Baby." I was on the edge of my seat ... EVERY TIME!

And why are we drawn? Because we honor the effort. The older I get, the more respect I have for that one little attribute - EFFORT! When we see an injustice that plots a David against a Goliath, or when we perceive that there is an advantaged opponent, we can empathize, and the underdog gets our vote every time. There is a caveat, however, which is that they must appear deserving of the win. It would be a completely different story if there was no effort put forth. What if Ralph Macchio had put in no training whatsoever and had instead threw his hands in and decided to simply bribe the judges in order to pull out the win. I somehow think it would have gone straight to DVD!

What if Rocky, rather than run up the 72 stone steps of the Philadelphia Museum of Arts listening to the *Eye of the Tiger*, instead hired a hitman to take out his opponent? There would likely not have been 24 more Rockies made after that (I lost track). There's just something about a hard-working, worthy underdog that brings out emotion in each of us.

It's the effort that we love. It's the struggle that we admire. It's the resolute dedication that inspires us, especially when success seems to be against all the odds. It stirs something in our souls and reminds us that anything is possible. Second chances are possible. New beginnings and fresh starts are possible. CHANGE suddenly becomes POSSIBLE!

Yes, there are things in life that we cannot control, and yes, change is likely inevitable. However, embracing change DOES NOT simply mean throwing in the towel and giving up. If there are things in your life that need changing, THEN CHANGE THEM. If you have a commute that you dread, or a job that seems to be draining the very life out of you, THEN CHANGE IT. If you are in a relationship that is toxic, stifling, or heaven-forbid abusive, then CHANGE IT. This is part of what it means to EMBRACE CHANGE. To know that life does not need to be hard ALL OF THE TIME. You have the power to create the life that you choose! You have the power to advance and adjust along the way! While positive change takes EFFORT, it will make your success that much sweeter.

Always Seek Correction

Many years ago, a friend told me about one of the most important work projects he had ever been a part of. He was working with a multi-billion-dollar, multi-national company remaking their core software product. This software was designed to help millions of users every month. Its success was critical to the health of the organization and its customers.

His team worked for many months to understand users' problems. They designed and built and tested new innovations. They did this for over a year before presenting it to the company's board. When it was finally finished and ready to launch, they called for a meeting to present the new and improved software.

The senior project manager, I'll call him Tim, was sent to represent the entire team. He would represent the tens of thousands of hours of skilled work by hundreds of talented people. They had gone through everything with a fine-toothed comb. They had given it their all. They were excited and confident. They had nailed it.

The board members assembled and were of diverse backgrounds and experience. They were highly skilled in growing and sustaining healthy companies. Tim was slightly intimidated by the success of those that had gathered, but he was excited to showcase his team's achievements.

The senior member of the board stood to introduce the presentation. It was brief; "We're here to review changes to the software. Now, let's find everything wrong with it."

Tim's heart seemed to both sink and implode from the statement. "Everything wrong with it!? Nothing is wrong with it!" he aggressively thought.

That same senior board member then put his hand on the project manager's shoulder. He calmly said with a soft smile, "Always seek for correction."

Tim then presented the new software. The board asked many questions and made even more comments.

Something miraculous happened.

Dozens upon dozens of now-glaring errors in the software were exposed. Holes in the flow and user experience were brought to light.

They had found *everything* wrong with it.

Tim left the meeting that day humbled and awestruck. A lesson he would never forget. Seeking for correction had allowed him to be more successful than he could have ever been without it. The software, and the team that built it, could now be more successful and helpful because of this experience. They made the needed corrections and the software was a smashing success. To this day it is used by millions of people around the world.

Something undesirable had remained hidden. Until correction was sought for, it would have remained hidden and unrefined. Never reaching its fullest potential.

We improve by doing, reviewing, seeking for the corrections, adjusting, and doing again.

Always seek for correction.

Or Don't …

I know that I just shared with you the importance of seeking correction, and while I strongly believe in that principle, sometimes seeking change is not the answer at all. Sometimes, in an effort to find happiness, we seek for changes, but what we really need is a change in perspective. What we really need is to find gratitude in our abundance.

We live in an era where there seems to be a pervading dissatisfaction with life. Social scientists conduct yearly polls to analyze the happiness of Americans. Every year, Gallup interviews more than 160,000 adults in the United States and asks them about their sense of purpose, their social relationships, their financial security, their health, and their connectedness to their community. Sadly, the most recent findings show that only 31% of Americans would consider themselves happy.

Why is this? In a country that could arguably be considered one of the most prosperous countries in the world, why is it that a majority of them are "dissatisfied?" Is it possible that sometimes having so much can be blinding?

How would you feel if you lost everything? Think about it honestly. Think of all the things that mean the absolute most to you in this world, and then picture them all gone tomorrow. Too many people live with everything they need (and more) but they simply can't see it. The thought of losing their job, a spouse, or even freedom are terrifying, yet often, in the day to day grind of life, they forget to recognize these as the blessing that they are. Ironically enough these tend to be the same areas where they focus on things that are wrong.

Many of us have safety, security, and strong relationships, yet happiness still seems to evade us. What is missing? May I suggest it's possible that nothing is missing. More money, nicer clothes, a better job, a bigger house, or even a different spouse may NOT be the problem. Is it possible that by failing to see all that we have, we continue to search for what will never fulfill us? Surprisingly, sometimes nothing actually needs to change. Perspective can be everything, and only you have power to control that. Working for a perspective fueled by gratitude may be the only missing piece of the puzzle. Perspective can change everything without anything really changing. We must learn to find gratitude in where we are while at the same time pushing forward to continually be creating the life that we choose.

Emotions vs Feelings

A part of building a life of meaning, purpose, and fulfillment includes the ability to change our feelings. Brendon Bruchard is one of my favorite author-teachers. For me, an element of a great teacher is someone who has overcome a challenge, learned a powerful lesson from it, and then shared that lesson with others. The challenge can be simple, but the lesson can be so profound that it can make a shift inside of me. That was the case with Brendon. In his book "High-Performance Habits," he opened my eyes to a concept that had always been a part of me, but something that I couldn't quite identify. Almost like when you first look through a pair of binoculars. You have a rough idea of what you are looking at, but the moment you adjust the focus, suddenly you can see things with perfect clarity. This is the clarity that came when I understood the difference between emotions and feelings.

Emotions are something that come and go. They can be triggered by a variety of different things. Sometimes a sound can bring an emotion (like alarm when hearing ambulance sirens), sometimes a certain smell can evoke emotions (like comfort when smelling fresh baked bread), and sometimes our hormones can run our emotions amok (ladies you know what I'm talking about). As I've paid closer attention to my emotions, I've been able to notice small situations that can trigger emotion in me. An overflowing kitchen garbage (frustration), sitting in traffic (agitation), a sweet text (appreciation), a grey winter day (gloominess), a hug from my husband or kids (love). You get the picture. Emotions are temporary and they come and go throughout our day.

Feelings on the other hand are more concrete. They linger and can have a lasting impact on not only our day, but on our very character. Now here's the most powerful lesson, I hope you're paying attention, because this is profound and I won't say that many profound things in this book. So here it is: WE CHOOSE OUR FEELINGS! WE DO! No one else on the planet has the power to decide how we feel.

Sure, others can have a tremendous impact on the emotions that we experience, but only we can choose how to feel.

When Dan was first diagnosed with cancer, I would wake up every morning, and within seconds realize that it was not a dream. Each day I would experience the same dread, fear, and deep sorrow—the kind that makes you think you might throw up. It was awful. In the beginning I didn't know how to shake it. I would go into robot mode and simply allow these emotions to circle me for the entire day. Quickly, however, I realized that this was an awful way to live, and an awful way to FEEL. I knew that we were dealing with something difficult, but I also knew that these emotions would not help us in the battle that we were now asked to fight. And so little by little I began to evaluate my emotions each morning and then make a conscious effort to decide how to feel! Luckily Dan is a naturally optimistic guy and is always looking for the fun things in life. I still remember the morning he said, "Babe, give me a kiss, our future is so bright!" Hard to feel glum around a person like that, right!

My experiences have brought me just about every emotion imaginable. But I have discovered the power in recognizing that I can still choose how I FEEL! I have learned to pause, look at the emotions that I am experiencing and then DECIDE if that's how I WANT to feel. I'm not saying it's EASY...some days wiping away the tears to choose joy can take everything you've got! I'm also not referring to grief here. Grief is an entirely different beast that can drop in like an unexpected visitor. Grief requires endurance, self-love, and a significant amount of patience. But living a happy life is about DECIDING to live a happy life. Even on our hardest days, we still have the opportunity to choose how we want to feel.

As I have tried to really hone in on this skill it has changed my life. I'm not being dramatic when I say that. It has truly been life-altering. I now have a morning routine where I begin each day by intentionally choosing a feeling for that day. It's not right when I wake up, usually after the gym, and after I've gotten the kids off to school. But I take a few minutes each day, and I WRITE down how I choose to FEEL that day. Sometimes it's joyful, or cheerful, and sometimes it's calm, or grateful. Bold, brave, productive, determined, loved, faithful, kind, generous...these have all been "Feelings-Of-The-Day" and it is honestly one of the greatest practices that I have learned. To be confronted with a lousy day, or some negative emotions (that might be perfectly justified mind you), and to then have the power TO CHANGE how you FEEL... now that's powerful!! Like I already mentioned, if you don't like it CHANGE IT! The best place to practice that is with the emotions that are not serving you. You have the power to change them!

Please keep in mind that there are always going to be exceptions to this. Grief, for example, can feel like a complete tidal wave and can come at the most unexpected times. These types of emotions often take patience and time to manage. I am also not referring to depression or mental illness, either. I have tremendous empathy for those who are dealing with those types of situations. And you deserve all the love and compassion in the world. But my hope is that, even in your darkest days, you can cling to at least the DESIRE to choose happiness and the HOPE that somehow, in some way, it will grace your heart and your home again. And on that note, I feel it is worth saying that I hope you are taking whatever steps might be necessary to create any CHANGE that you may need in your life. If that's speaking with a professional, changing your medication, cleaning up your diet, or getting some exercise (all proven to help) I hope you are at least doing SOMETHING. I think I can speak for most people when I say, that helping others comes a little easier when people are at least trying to help themselves!

Power in Surrender

I can't finish this chapter without sharing one more truth about change. And that is that there are simply some things that we can never change. There are some things in life that will force change upon us, while there are other changes in life that we will actively pursue. But sometimes, there is nothing that we can do to create a change. There are mountains that we cannot move, no matter how hard we try or how much we want that to happen. There are miscarriages that we can't control, in-laws we can't escape, colleagues that we can't avoid, those friends that always keep us waiting, and awful cat videos that your grandparents love to forward. There are simply some situations, that while we would love to change, we simply must accept.

It reminds me of the serenity prayer of Alcoholics Anonymous: "God, grant me the serenity to *accept the things I cannot change*, the courage to change the things I can, and the wisdom to know the difference." I love the idea of "serenity" that this mindset can bring. There is a peace and a calm that comes when we learn to surrender to the things that we cannot change. What are the things in your life that you would do anything to change? Are you spending time, or worse, energy, on strategizing a plan on how to change something you likely will never be able to change? Are there things that maybe you could quietly let go? Are there changes that need to be made in YOU that can allow you to better accept others exactly where they are?

In the moments that we cannot change, even then, we must CHOOSE happiness anyway!

PRACTICAL TOOLS to Embrace Change:

1. **Understand that change is inevitable.** When you understand that life simply cannot stay the same forever, you can begin to anticipate change before it catches you off guard. Being prepared, and having the confidence that you will make it through (resilience), can make for much smoother sailing. And remember that self-loathing or the blame game are counterproductive. As you stay focused, you will learn that embracing change becomes easier and easier.

2. **Adjust your attitude.** There are some things in life that we have no control over. Our height, the weather, delayed flights, or the longevity of our appliances (random I know, but my water-heater just went out.....ugh). Life can be incredible and exhilarating, but it can also be fraught with difficult challenges that seem destined to ruin you. In these situations, we really only have control over one thing: our attitudes. And attitude is EVERYTHING! Dancing in the rain is much better than crying about the storm.

3. **Doubt and uncertainty are NORMAL.** Any change, whether unexpected or initiated, can feel daunting and scary. It is likely that there will never be a time when you are completely absent of these thoughts and emotions. You are human after all and it's completely normal

to fear the unfamiliar. Don't waste any time wondering if something is wrong with you if you hate change. Don't try to resist change, simply learn to act anyway—regardless of the uncertainty.

4. **Be open-minded.** Change does not need to be overwhelming. Rather than seeing change as something to fear or dread, try to see it as a new adventure or something that has the potential to improve you or your life. Don't just sit and wait for bad things to go away, instead develop a new perspective and take challenges head on. Remember that your response to any event, and not the event itself, is what determines the outcome you experience.

5. **Always seek correction.** Enough said. It can change your life.

CHAPTER 6

KNOW THE E.N.E.M.Y.

"Beware of no man more than of yourself; we carry our worst enemies within us."

- Charles Spurgeon

You are designed to be great! I wish I could gather you in my kitchen, serve you some warm bread, and tell you just how smart, capable, and wise you are. I wish I could magically unlock your hidden potential and present it to your mind's eye. I wish I could reveal your inner strengths and show you the many purposes you have yet to accomplish. And when I was done with that, I would warn you that living a life of meaning and becoming who you want to be will not be easy. I would share an important secret. You have an E.N.E.M.Y.

Within each of us are experiences, passions, talents, skills, desires, and dreams ... yet to be fulfilled. Why are they "yet to be fulfilled?" There's no simple answer for this, and it's likely because living a life of purpose takes hard work. But there's another factor at play and it's not something that we talk about very often. There is a real enemy lurking, whose exact goal is to prevent us from being everything that we are meant to become!

The Real ENEMY

Since we have already learned one lesson from Isaac Newton, it's appropriate that we allow him to teach us another lesson here. His Third Law of Motion is perfect for understanding this skill. This law states that for every action there is an equal and opposite reaction. His theory is in reference to physics, but it is just as applicable here. The universe is not indifferent to your progression, and the sooner you recognize that, the sooner you will be able to combat it.

Steven Pressfield articulated it best, "When you and I set out to create anything—art, commerce, science, love—or to advance in the directions of a higher, nobler, version of ourselves, we uncork from the universe, ineluctably, an equal and opposite reaction."

Our souls crave progress, and as we advance in life, whether in giant ways or in tiny, almost imperceptible steps, we begin to live our purpose. It's in these moments of progress that the enemy shows up. You see as we put forth our effort to improve and take a step in the right direction, like Newton explained, there is an opposite reaction that I call the ENEMY.

So what is this ENEMY?

Here it is.

E - every

N - narrative that

E - excuses

M- mastering

Y- yourself

EVERY NARRATIVE that EXCUSES MASTERING YOURSELF

That's the real ENEMY! It's the tireless, relentless, malignant chatter in our own minds that time and time again cause us to doubt and falter. It's the voice that sounds like our own, and that creates stories in our mind convincing us to "back down," to cower, and to somehow become less than we are destined to become.

As I have mentioned before, this life is NOT a dress rehearsal! You get ONE shot to make it great! And one of the most important skills you will ever learn is the skill of self-mastery. The ability to be exactly who YOU want to be because YOU have mastered YOU. To be able to be in the mood that YOU decide, to control your own thoughts, your own appetites, and your own passions. To fully develop your talents and control the constant banter in your mind. To be completely in charge of WHO YOU WANT TO BE! That will be one of the greatest accomplishments of your life. It will begin with vision, but it will endure because of persistence and perseverance. Your ability to rise will be determined by your ability to combat the enemy.

Unfortunately, it won't be easy.

There is an old saying, "Keep your friends close but your enemies closer." Understanding the enemy will always keep you one step ahead of the game. This enemy shows up everyday, seems to know you almost better than you know yourself, and is so sly, so cunning, and so tricky that it is often hard to detect. The enemy doesn't take a break, doesn't get holidays off (oh especially not holidays), and has probably ruined more lives than the plague (ok maybe I'm being a little dramatic, but you get the point).

There is in existence a sort of "personal gravity" - a force, an opposition, a resistance that will pull you down and keep you from elevating yourself to a higher plane. I have witnessed this so many times in my own life, and in the lives of others around me. If you are living as your most base self, you will likely not experience any of the effects of personal gravity. For example, if you have zero desire to get into shape, to write a book, to work for that next promotion, or zero desire to be anything other than what you are right now, then this idea of personal gravity won't make sense to you. It's not until you aspire to achieve more, to do more, to serve more, or in any way shape or form to BECOME more, that you will feel the resistance of this gravity in your life.

Every single thought, story, and narrative that comes into your mind, that prevents you from self-mastery and personal growth, is the enemy that you need to fight every day. It is these stories that penetrate the mind; thoughts that originate as seeds that can grow to be debilitating beliefs. Beliefs become actions, and of course, our actions determine our destiny. Sounds a little cliché, right?

It's not. It's very real and can have a very real impact on a life meant for greatness. You will feel it the strongest right as you are about to elevate to the next level. I've experienced this enemy so many times, and once, it was so powerful, I almost became convinced that the narrative was my own.

Roughly seven years before Dan was ever diagnosed with cancer, I had been led to study disease prevention and nutrition. I use the word "led" only so that I don't come across too crazy. But the truth is that it was so much more than that. It was almost as if there was someone else inside of me constantly urging me (or more like hounding me) to learn absolutely everything I could about the links between diet and disease. I became a little obsessed. I tried to glean knowledge from every source I could find. I read incessantly on the topic. My nightstand was overflowing with books, and after a long day with the kids, I would exhaustively crawl into bed, but then become alive as I devoured the information in the books. Cancer, along with many other diseases, became a nightly study, as did nutrition and global dietary patterns. My brain was like a sponge taking it all in. This went on for almost three years.

I had learned so much and was eager to share my passions and my new-found knowledge. I wasn't sure where to start, so I began a small business doing in-home cooking classes to groups of people. I wanted to show others, in a hands-on way, that eating healthy could be easy and delicious. I decided to take it one-step further and apply to become what is known as a "Food for Life Instructor" organized by the Physicians Committee for Responsible Medicine. This is an organization that selects and trains only a handful of people each year (it has since expanded significantly). Many from Utah had applied in the past but none had been selected.

As I looked over the application process, it became clear that they were looking for someone much more qualified than I was. They asked about a medical degree, a nursing background, or culinary training. Nope, nope, and nope. I was immediately intimidated, but not dissuaded. I was still on fire at this point, and

I knew that this was the next step on my path. I KNEW IT, I just needed them to know it.

So I filled out the application and submitted the required demo video (which was so daunting, and now when I watch it back on YouTube can see that it wasn't really very good). I was worried that they still might need a little more persuasion, so I included an additional plea in the form of an essay titled, "I'm the girl you are looking for." I desperately wrote, explaining to them that what I lacked in technical experience, I well made up for in passion! I hit submit. And then I waited.

The day I got the call was absolutely euphoric! I had been selected and I couldn't believe it (although deep down I JUST KNEW that this was for me). I was going to fly out to Washington to be trained with the other selectees from around the country. I was ecstatic and squealed around the house, throwing my kids in the air.

But something interesting happened in Washington.

From almost the moment I arrived, the narratives began.

You don't really belong here. You're clearly not as trained as the others that are here. Initially I was able to silence these thoughts with the pure adrenaline of being on a path that I felt divinely placed on. I was so excited to be

159

there and was committed to trying to encourage others to live a healthy life!

Unfortunately, the excitement didn't last long. I distinctly remember the plane ride home, and the barrage of thoughts that filled my mind. They seemed to be loaded and triggered so that one thought would come right after another. *You've always said your kids were your first priority. Your children are still young. They need you. Are you a mother first or are you a hypocrite?* I scarcely had the chance to shield off one before another thought was hurled my way. *Who are YOU to teach people about nutrition? What do you really know anyway? You're clearly not thin enough. No one will listen to you. People don't listen to fat girls. You've just wasted your time and your money, and you know it.*

At this time in my life I wasn't as distinctly aware of the enemy as I am now. I couldn't recognize these narratives as a form of resistance, designed to keep me from progressing. I didn't understand this type of gravity that was pulling me down. Truthfully, it felt fairly natural. Like my own voice, simply offering me clarity and reason. Helping me see the mistake that I had made and rationalizing with me to get "back on track".

And I succumbed.

I returned home, and apologetically told my husband that I had decided that the time wasn't quite right. The kids were in a busy stage of life, and I could pursue this dream later. They deserved a mom that wasn't distracted. They needed me. He needed me! He sat there stunned, but I reassured him that I mostly just wanted to see if I actually "could" do it, and that I was satisfied in just knowing that I had been selected.

I refrained from telling him that I had gotten on the scale right when I got home, and clearly (what should have been obvious to both us), I simply wasn't thin enough to teach people anything.

I have discovered that there is a darkness that can appear in one's life when they have consciously (or maybe even subconsciously) chosen to step off their path. When that path has been revealed, there is an inner voice that calls at first, pleading to echo the reminders of who you want to be. But sadly, it can be silenced quickly. Or even worse, numbed. And that inner plea can be so easily overshadowed by the ENEMY. Happily interjecting with the narratives that will keep you exactly where you are.

I experienced something that I had never experienced before. A sadness. A darkness. Depression. But I couldn't identify it. I felt "off," but gave flimsy excuses to myself as to the reasons. It was March, and it had been a long winter. I just needed some sunshine. Money was tight, that's all. The kids were a lot of work. We just had a lot going on. Not once in the months that followed did I think that what I was feeling had anything to do with chickening out on my life.

Months went by, and things started to get worse. I began to realize that something might be wrong with me. I usually had a zest for life, and it was completely gone. Normally an early bird, I now struggled to get out of bed. A stickler for rules and education, I now found myself driving the kids to school late, or letting them skip altogether. I felt a slow, subtle darkness begin to creep in. I wanted to numb it, chase it away, but instead I found myself welcoming it. This wasn't me, but truthfully, I didn't even know who "me" was anymore.

I wept to Dan that something was wrong with me. I was scared and I couldn't shake it. I told him I needed a break. From everything. To try and figure it out. I found myself getting in the car and driving to my secret place. A place I would go to reconnect with myself and my Maker. I sat and I sobbed. And then slowly I wiped my tears. And I began to think back on when I last remembered feeling happy. When I last had felt a joy for life, and excitement about getting up in the mornings. And of course, my thoughts brought me back to Washington D.C. What had happened? What had changed and created this shift inside of me?

One by one, I thought of all of the stories that I had told myself. In my mind's eye I looked at each one, almost as if to hold it in my hand and examine it from each angle. Turning them over, and slowly recognizing something. These thoughts weren't mine. Yes, they came TO me, but they were not FROM me. They looked foreign and felt cold. They had taken me from a place of progress and joy and had settled me in a place of stagnancy and now despair.

With this new knowledge, I suddenly felt powerful. I felt clarity that I hadn't seen in months. I felt a calm happiness begin to swell within me as I realized the lies that I had believed. As a young child, I had been taught that the opposite of a lie was a truth. This simple statement now had me starting to smile. Did that mean that I WAS qualified to teach; that I actually did have knowledge that I could use to help people? Did it mean that I could still be a good mother AND share my message with others? And that maybe, just maybe, my physical appearance had nothing to do with my skill set? It might sound absurd to you as a reader, but to me in that moment, it was as if the stars all aligned, the heavens parted and a double, no, a TRIPLE rainbow was now arching in the sky. I could suddenly SEE. I understood everything SO clearly. I was able to identify this enemy and all of the narratives that I had bought into.

I went on to become an active instructor of health and wellness. I taught cooking shows, lunch-and-learns, started a blog, had a small segment on the local morning news, and at last count had taught thousands of people about the importance of taking care of their bodies. I eventually got a master's degree in nutrition science (although the enemy showed up pretty heavily before that). Those narratives didn't ever really subside, but I learned to not give them any heed.

Tragedy

Now this narrative that I'm describing doesn't need to originate as your own thought. It could come from a teacher, a parent, a co-worker, or even a child. But regardless of the source, the narrative only takes hold when you allow it. So you'll need to show up to battle. Everyday. Because these narratives are powerful. Especially if these narratives have come from a tragedy. Sometimes those are the ones that will stay with you for life. Sometimes the ENEMY will use the most painful experiences to leave the loudest narrative.

As I'm writing this today there was a tragedy that happened in our small town of Riverton, Utah. A 16-year-old girl was driving her younger sister to school and upon turning left at a green light was struck by an oncoming car. Her sister who was in ninth grade at my son's school was life-flighted and unfortunately passed away. We didn't know the family personally, but we talked together as a family thinking of how easily it could have been my children. My 16-year-old daughter driving my ninth grader to school turning left at that exact same light. We pondered as a family what we could do to somehow reach out to this other family. We discussed sending flowers or a card or possibly some money. And this morning as I still keep thinking about this family my thoughts go to that sweet 16-year-old who will feel responsible for killing her sister. What could we tell her? Could we tell her that she was loved? That no one blamed her? That accidents happen. Could we tell her that we knew it was an accident and so did everybody else? My hope is that this sweet girl is continuously surrounded by people that love her. Telling her the things she needs to hear to help her heal. And my thoughts immediately went to the enemy. The real ENEMY. The narrative inside her head. What was the ENEMY whispering to her? This will have more of a stronghold on her than anything else. Her future and her success with be tied to her ability to fight the story that might be playing in her mind. I pray that, despite the tragedy, she will know that she is worthy of love and a life of happiness! I pray that she will master her thoughts and that they will be filled with nothing but love and encouragement.

Negative Narratives

You're not good enough. You don't belong. You're not smart enough, pretty enough, strong enough— these are narratives that are pretty easy to identify. And yet they are still powerful.

You can start tomorrow, you're too tired, you've been through a lot, you should sleep in, no one will notice, you don't know how—a few more that are fairly easy to spot yet can quickly provide the excuse we may we looking for.

Because there are endless numbers of people, with endless numbers of purposes, there are endless varieties of narratives. Some are so subtle, and so counterfeit that we often will never even recognize them until we are at the very edges of our comfort zone (which as we all know is where the greatest progress occurs).

What are your narratives? Do they come from your own head, or from the voices of other people in your life? Have you identified some of them? Are there others still lurking?

We must be aware that the ENEMY will focus not only on ourselves, but will include others in the various narratives that play in our mind. And they may look just as familiar. *They* are not good enough. *They* don't belong. *They* aren't smart enough etc. These types of thoughts, whether introspective or extrospective, are toxic and will do nothing to help you pursue a life of purpose and meaning. Comparison is another pernicious narrative and is a cunning thief of joy and progress that must be avoided.

We must learn to still the voices of skepticism and unnecessary criticism. Thoughts of insult and injury, prejudice and pessimism, serve no one. We must recognize that we become what we think about. Ralph Waldo Emerson said, "Sow a thought and you reap an action; sow an act and you reap a habit; sow a habit and you reap a character; sow a character and you reap a destiny." There is another popular saying, "you are the average of the five people you spend the most time with." I don't disagree, but the power of our mind is significantly more influential, and our thoughts will determine who we become more than anything else. Which is why it is so important to triumph over the ENEMY.

It's Not Them It's You

There's an old black and white photo of a horse race circulating the internet. The image shows two horses running neck in neck. As they approach the finish line, the horse on the left reaches out and bites the horse on the right. The one on the right goes on to win the race. The message propagating with the photo is that "a true champion has the determination to keep pushing forward when others would love to see you fail." It's a fine message, I guess. But in my experience, it's just not very accurate.

There are so many clichés out there that say something along the lines of "if someone is strong enough to bring you down, show them that you are strong enough to get up," or "whoever is trying to bring you down is already below you." Again, these are fine ... I guess. But I don't think they paint the right picture. If you really sit down and think about it, are there really people in your life that are trying to bring you down? Are there really people that are hoping you fail? Has anyone ever really said to you, "I knew you would never make it!"? Maybe for some of you that may be the case, but that is NOT the majority. This message conjures up an opponent that you really don't need to be concerned with. For most people their biggest enemy is NOT "other people" getting in the way of their success—it is THEMSELVES. And if we really want to get into the nitty-gritty, that obstacle looks a lot like laziness, indecision, being "lukewarm," undisciplined, unengaged, doubtful, fearful, etc. Learning to master yourself will be significantly more powerful than worrying about any naysayers that may (or may not) be lurking.

As we become more in tune with the ways that we limit ourselves, we soon realize that it's our thoughts more than anything else that sabotage our success. Not our circumstances, not our income, not our position, and likely not anyone ELSE. It's our thoughts, beliefs, and actions that are the catalyst for our outcomes.

Disguises

Sometimes the enemy doesn't seem like a narrative at all and can be disguised as all sorts of things. Discouragement, despair, and defeat are among these. Distraction is also a HUGE play for the enemy. Anything and everything that can be used as a simple tool to keep you from your greatest potential could be considered the enemy. Let's look at social media for just a moment. There may be plenty of positives that can come from using social media to connect with others, but one should be very wary of the opportunity cost that is paid. Opportunity cost is defined as "the loss of potential gain from other alternatives when one alternative is chosen." Time is one of your greatest assets, and when you choose time on social media, there is a loss of potential gain from using that time elsewhere. Most people complain that "not enough time" is likely the biggest culprit for them not accomplishing their heartfelt goals. If time is an issue for you, the little minutes of "distraction" can easily add up.

Another form of distraction, and one that I have often fallen prey to, is the feeling that you need to learn more before you can act. One wouldn't automatically think that there is anything inherently wrong with the desire to gain more knowledge, but mark my words, it can be a tool of the ENEMY. Of course, there is absolutely nothing intrinsically wrong with actively pursuing learning, in fact, it is a sign of a great leader. However, there could be a narrative behind the "seeking" that is subtly inhibiting action. Let's say that there is something that you would like to achieve, and maybe you don't feel quite educated enough to accomplish it. Perhaps you want to start a website, create an online course, or something simpler like learning photography. You start the process by finding resources to help you learn how to do whatever it is that you would like to do. Maybe you check some books out of the library, listen to a podcast on the subject, or take a class to teach you how to move forward. This is fantastic as long as the narrative does not convince you that you are never ready, and that you always need to learn a little more, research just a bit further, gather just a few more things ... and then you'll get started. You can become so absorbed by the learning that you never actually implement any of the newly found knowledge. Interestingly, the learning is often not nearly as difficult as the applying. Perpetually staying in the "learning phase" is a safe and possibly even noble place to be, but if you're not careful it can be a trap. It's much easier to be a hearer of the word rather than a doer. True success comes from the progressive achievement of a goal, and that goal requires action. Certainly, learning has an important role to play, but it must never distract us from the actual accomplishing. Once again, the narrative should never be an excuse to avoid the work.

Rachel Hollis

The Enemy can also show up looking a lot like jealousy, laziness, complaining, vanity etc. Have you ever come across someone successful and thought to yourself, "Ya, I just don't like them?" You may have valid reasons for this, but if you take the time to really ask yourself "why" you don't like them, you might be surprised to find the dreaded Enemy subtly at work. Here's why. When someone has mastered something that you know intuitively that you should have mastered, or wished you would have mastered, there is a subconscious aversion to that person. They are a reminder to you of what you should be, AND COULD BE! Yet for reasons known or unknown, you have not achieved that level of mastery and it leaves you feeling "less than." I'll pick on women for a minute, because for some reason we have become masters at this. We may see a fit, pretty woman, and instantly not "like her." Is it because she has misbehaved, or offended us in some way? Or is it because she has learned to master her body or manage her time, or control her temper … or whatever! Somehow that triggers a reminder in us that we aren't exactly where we want to be ourselves. I've seen this time and time again, and most recently I've seen this with ME! I'm embarrassed to admit it, but the enemy snuck its way in, and the innocent bystander was Rachel Hollis. Oh Rachel, I cringe telling this story.

For those of who you don't know who Rachel Hollis is, and my guess is that by the time this book is published EVERYONE will know who Rachel is, I'll fill you in. She's a beautiful, spunky, small but fierce firecracker of a woman who is taking the world by storm! She started as an event planner and then built a multi-million-dollar empire with just a high school degree and a lot of grit. She is happily married, has four kids and a beautiful house. When I first heard of Rachel, I was participating in my very first weekend training on how to become a professional public speaker. "You haven't heard of Rachel Hollis?" I kept hearing. "Wow, she's everywhere and is one of the top female speakers in the country!" Great, I thought. And not in the "oh-awesome-for-her-she-probably-worked-hard-for-all-that-success" tone. It was more of "well-if-she-already-has-such-a-big-piece-of-this-pie-then-there-won't-be-enough-left-for-me" sort of a tone (notice the narrative already). That's the scarcity tone and if there were a scarcity emoji, then it would be the most used emoji by the enemy.

I went home that weekend and started casually "checking out" this Rachel chick. Ugh you can even FEEL my intention in that sentence. It wasn't to leave her an uplifting DM on Instagram, or to go and buy her latest book. it was to "check out" the competition. Gross! Now to be totally fair, I had no idea I was doing this at the time. Insecurities can be pretty darn deceptive. At the time, I thought I was just innocently "learning about the industry." I started following her, and after scrolling for a bit, I thought, yeah, she kind of bugs me. Rachel if you ever read this, I am totally ashamed of my childish reaction. This is the EXACT thing that girls get a bad rap for and I totally fell into the trap! I deserve to be tarred and feathered! I looked at her website, and put her book on hold at the library—which I had to wait three months to get because I didn't want to buy the book in case she bugged me (I'm disgusting, I know, but give me a minute to try and redeem myself).

I waited the three months, and in the meantime, I continued to read her posts, watch her stories, and signed up to receive her emails. Which were all, I slowly admitted, pretty darn good. And beneficial. To me. In my life. And then I started reading her book. I laughed out loud (she's funny), my heart ached with her horrific foster experience, I could totally relate to her body image, and I blushed and then told my girlfriends about her sex chapter. When I was done, I thought, wow, this Rachel Hollis is one heck of a lady. And business tycoon … and coach … and wife … and mother … and she's super cute. So what was my problem? All of IT! Every part of it. THAT was my problem. She had already accomplished the things in her life that I WANTED to accomplish. She was a big fancy shiny mirror reflecting my own inadequacies and a reminder of what I had not yet done!

Jealousy and envy can be the most subtle, and vilest, of the enemy's tools. Rachel had worked hard and lost the weight, she had hustled through and built a beautiful brand, she was out there showing up, every day, to offer service and inspiration to the world! And THAT is why she bugged me. Because it was ALL about ME! And let me tell you, that's a lousy place to be! This world does not need one more single person making their life all about THEM! Here was a woman that deserved nothing but my praise and encouragement, and all I could muster was a pathetic "she bugs me." Well guess what Rachel Hollis, I think you're fantastic! In fact, from this moment on I am going to leave nice comments, and thumbs up, and tell the people I know that I think what you've accomplished in life is pretty amazing. Not because YOU need it, but because I need it. And rather than use your example to snuff out my little, small, barely-there, flicker of a light, I will use it as incredible inspiration, to ignite my own flame, and fuel to become who I want to be. Not Rachel, just Charity!

If you find yourself easily offended by the actions of others, it may be an indicator that you are unsatisfied with something that you wish you had more control of or need to work a little harder on. Like I mentioned earlier, our souls crave progress and can also identify progress in others. We could use it to take offense, or use it as inspiration, motivation, and fuel for our individual fires. Seeing other people living a dream that could easily be ours can be a pretty bitter pill to swallow. But luckily, it's never too late to realign and restart. It's never too late to master ourselves and achieve the success we are looking for!

An Enemy to the E.N.E.M.Y.

The good news is that the enemy is not all-powerful. There are ways to fight back, and If I had to select one thing that can combat the powers of the enemy faster than anything else, it would be learning to master your body. Have you heard of keystone habits? These are not like ordinary habits; these are more like super-hero habits. These are special habits, because as you master these, other areas of your life begin to improve as well. In the incredible book "The Power of Habit" Charles Duhigg describes these habits as the ones that can transform us because they can create "chain reactions that help other good habits take hold." They essentially have a ripple effect that spills over into the rest of our lives. Exercise is one of those keystone habits.

Duhigg further explains, "When people start habitually exercising, even as infrequently as once a week, they start changing other, unrelated patterns in their lives, often unknowingly. Typically, people who exercise start eating better and becoming more productive at work. They use credit cards less frequently and say they feel less stressed."

175

So here's the takeaway: if you want help in living your best life, living a happy life that, even with ups and downs, is filled with purpose, a great place to start is to make sure you are exercising! If this is something you are already doing, then cheers to you. You will likely confirm that this is a positive and beneficial practice in your life.

If, however you are NOT, then we need to have a little chat. This is the part where I might tell you all of the reasons why exercise is good for your heart and good for your brain and leads to a longer life. Or the part where I might remind you that along with only getting one life, you only get one body, so you darn well better take care of it. This might be the part where I start getting a little fired up thinking of my husband who is fighting for his life right now and I don't want to hear any of your sorry excuses for why you can't take 20 minutes out of your blasted day to significantly improve your life. Because if you can master just that one thing, then think of all of the areas of your life that you can master. And as your body gets stronger, your mind gets stronger, and when your mind is stronger, the enemy has less power—and suddenly you are right back on course to becoming incredible and changing lives, starting with your own!!!!! (Big breath, small sigh).

Or this might be the part where I soften just a little bit and remember that new habits can be hard, and simply encourage you, or rather beg you, to please make this a part of your life. And I'll remind you that you can choose ANY form of exercise that you like, even walking, though I'd be happier if you at least broke a sweat. But OK, fine, just start somewhere. But since it's likely that you already know ALL of this information, I'm just not going to go into a tirade about exercise. And as much as I really, REALLY, want to get into diet and nutrition, and talk about how what you eat actually has the ability to help you or hinder you on your path, I think I'll save that for another book.

So how about we just agree that fighting the narratives, and mastering yourself can be a pretty tough battle, and exercise can help with that battle. There are countless reasons why we should exercise, and just as many reasons why it's hard to make it a habit, but if you only needed one reason, it would be to help you learn to master yourself so that you can go on to master all the other things that you were meant to achieve in this life!

Let me close on a positive note. The good news is that just as the ENEMY most certainly exists, so too is there a force in the universe cheering you on and rallying to help you achieve everything that this life has to offer. Some call it manifesting, some call it "the secret," others call it a higher Power of God. Regardless of your beliefs, tapping into that positivity is available to us all and, in the end, is infinitely more powerful than the ENEMY.

Don't give up what you want most for something that you want right now!

PRACTICAL TOOLS to fight the E.N.E.M.Y.:

1. **Stay on Duty.** Learn to watch for and detect the ENEMY. Overtime you will be able to recognize the narratives that are playing in your mind. Remember that the enemy is designed to somehow, some way, leave you feeling less than, not enough, or simply in a negative space. When you notice any of these feelings, go deeper and try to find the narratives that preceded them.

2. **Find the Lie.** As soon as you have identified the Enemy, walk through the narrative (and yes, there is always a narrative, it just might take layers of digging). As soon as you have found the narrative, you'll be able to separate the truth from the lie. Here's an example: "As much as I would love to get back into shape, I simply don't have time to work out." That's the narrative, now let's take a peek. The truth is

that yes, you would in fact like to be in better shape and have more control of your body, but there's a powerful underlying lie here too. And that's that you don't have time. We all have 24 hours in a day. Which means you absolutely have "time." It's simply a matter of priority. That's the truth.

3. **Ask someone else**. As much as we wish we could see the ENEMY clearly, and as much as we wish we could identify the areas that need more self-mastery, the truth is that these things aren't always self-evident. However, those that know us best can often see our weaker points a little more clearly than we can. It takes a level of humility, but sometimes asking a trusted friend (with a solid foundation of love and compassion), is just what we need to help us identify the ENEMY in our lives.

4. **Earn Your Own Trust.** The first step in developing true self-mastery is being able to truly trust YOURSELF. This means that if you say you're going to do something that you do it. 100% of the time. In order to really show up in your life, you first need to master showing up for yourself. This is critical to your progress. If you haven't fully earned your own trust, it's not too late to start. And you can start small. For example, you can give yourself small tasks

to accomplish and then make sure you follow through. Clean a closet for 5 minutes, floss before bed, return 5 emails, turn off your phone for 30 minutes. It really doesn't matter what it is ... as long as you follow through! You must become your main master.

5. **Tell good stories about others**. This technique has a double bonus. The first is the Pygmalion effect. You can shape other people's performance for the better when you have higher expectations of them. But there's something in it for you too! As you practice telling good stories, even just in your own head, about your spouse, your boss, your colleagues, or your friends, you'll find that the stories you're telling yourself will change too.

CHAPTER 7

BECOME A MULTIPLIER; the Art of Creation

"Don't ask what the world needs. Ask what makes you come alive and go do it. Because what the world needs is more people who have come alive."

- Howard Thurman

The idea of being a multiplier came from a fabulous book of the same name by Liz Wiseman. She delves into two different types of management styles, the first being a Multiplier, and the second being a Diminisher. Her experience and research found that Multipliers have a way of using their talents to amplify the intelligence and even increase the capabilities of those that they lead. "People got smarter and better in their presence. Ideas grew, challenges were surmounted, hard problems were solved," she explained. Diminishers on the other hand, seem to drain and even shut down the skills of those around them. For these "leaders," the focus on their own knowledge, and "their resolve to be the smartest person in the room had a diminishing effect on everyone else."

Wiseman goes on to conclude that "in studying Multipliers and Diminishers, we learned that at the most fundamental level, they get dramatically different results from their people, they hold a different logic and set of assumptions about people's intelligence, and they do a small number of things very differently."

So what were some of these differences? What set a Multiplier apart from a Diminisher? I was eager to take a deeper look and determine where on the spectrum I fell.

I was disappointed with my findings.

As I took a closer look at how Wiseman would describe a Diminisher, I saw more of myself than I would like to admit. To begin with, Diminishers look at the intellect of those around them in a sort of "they will never figure this out without me" kind of a way. Enter my four children, and loving husband, all nodding in unison and pointing directly at me. Fine, guilty of that one. Another distinction is how Diminishers set direction, make decisions, and get things done. This is accomplished through "telling," "deciding," and jumping in to take control. Ugh! Guilty, guilty, guilty.

Multipliers on the other hand see things differently, and typically think that people are smart and will figure things out. They steer direction by helping to develop talent, and rather than taking control they consult others before making final decisions. They also creatively seek for group support in order to get things done rather than try to command everything themselves.

From the viewpoint of how I raise my children, how I behave in my marriage, and how I lead the team at Silver Fern, I was sad to see that I certainly leaned more towards a Diminisher than I wished! In my defense, I'm a go-getter, a type A-personality, and a bit of a control freak (ok maybe more than a bit). I love personal development and I live on a tight schedule. But my discovery helped me to see that typically only one person benefits from these characteristics and that person is me. I'm pretty sure that God didn't send me here to just elevate myself! So with some humility and a lot of effort, I have been able to make some changes.

The principle of being a multiplier in Wiseman's terms is about finding ways to bring out the best in other people. It's about using the resources and talents that are currently available, and simply finding ways to do it better. The seventh and final skill I want to share with you includes this concept but takes it a step further and a little deeper. What if you could stretch yourself in a way, to use the tools that you already have, and make something more? What if you had the ability to bring something into existence that wasn't there before? In essence, what if you could become a creator? The last skill in this book is all about being a multiplier, avoiding the scarcity mindset and ultimately becoming a creator. It's about using your own unique gifts, talents, experiences, and insights to develop something that wouldn't exist without you...and then to lead others to do the same.

It Starts in The Mind

I wouldn't say I grew up poor, but I certainly wouldn't say I grew up rich either. With six kids in the family, living on a middle-class income, I would say we were happy but not wealthy. We always had "enough," but I certainly didn't feel like there was ever excess. For many of us, our mindset towards money is often formed in our childhood. It was no different for me. I developed the belief that it was honorable and necessary to become self-sufficient and to work hard to provide for the necessities of life. But along with that belief, for some reason I also adopted the feeling that, while it was honorable to "get by" it was wrong to work to "get ahead" or to have excess. To have nice things, a large home, fancy cars, or luxurious vacations was all a little too indulgent. Money was evil—or at least that's what I thought. Besides, there wasn't really "enough" of those things to go around. The only people that actually achieved that level of wealth likely had to give up something else to get there. And even worse was that their level of wealth probably meant that someone else was left living with less.

This is what I believed, and it was years before I discovered that this way of thinking actually had a name! It had been studied, well-documented, and written about for decades! I had no idea that it was even a "thing." But it apparently it is, and it is called the scarcity mindset!

I'm sure many of you are already familiar with this way of thinking, but for those of you who aren't, I'll elaborate. The easiest way for me to do that is to use a pie. It's' how I learned the concept, it's easy to comprehend, and pie is delicious! Stephen Covey taught me this principle in his book *"The 7 Habits of Highly Effective People."* Here's what he said about it: *"Most people are deeply scripted in what I call the Scarcity Mentality. They see life as having only so much, as though there were only one pie out there. And if someone were to get a big piece of the pie, it would mean less for everybody else."*

I bought into that way of thinking hook, line, and sinker! I believed that I just needed to be content with whatever slice I was served and that I must simply accept my lot in life. In fact, I should take it one step further and find virtue and honor in frugality and prudence. I could find nobility in shunning the "finer things" of life and finding appreciation for my little piece of pie.

But there is a problem with that way of thinking. A lot of problems actually! The three biggest being fear, lost opportunity, and selfishness. To begin with, scarcity thinking is essentially another way that fear seeps into our lives. We must never ever take counsel from our fears. Yes, tough things might happen in life, and yes, that may temporarily lead to a lack of resources. But living in fear is not a way to live. Besides, by now you've built up the resilience to know that there is nothing you can't handle. In addition to the element of fear, the scarcity mindset goes contrary to the laws of the universe. If we look carefully, we can see the message of abundance scattered all throughout the universe. The stars in the sky are innumerable. Every blade of grass and every sand in the sea bears witness of the abundance all around us. We live in the most prosperous time in the history of the planet (despite people's fears of diminishing resources). We must learn to believe in the abundance that surrounds us and believe that we are entitled to as much or as little of that abundance as we desire.

Which brings me to another "abundant" law of nature—but this one has some strings attached. This law is the Law of the Harvest. You reap what you sow. If you sow generously, you reap generously, but if you sow sparingly, you reap sparingly. This is part of the American dream and it's the idea that there are no limits to what you can achieve and acquire. It's important that your heart is set in the right place, and by now you understand that "things" are not the only answer for happiness. But even if your heart "isn't right." the Law of the Harvest still applies. The only strings attached are the efforts required on your part. There are no free rides here. But using your skills and hard work, not only can you have as much "pie" as you want, you can also help to fill the needs of others.

Which brings me to my final point in the detriments of scarcity thinking—no one else is served. Not only is this mindset centered in fear, but it is also centered in "self." It took me years to realize that in always worrying about whether or not I would have enough, I never took time to wonder how I could help anyone else. Not only was *I* not being served but no one else was being served either. It took a tremendous amount of practice and diligence to change my thinking. I finally realized that there are no "limits" and that if I accumulated wealth, I would be able to use that wealth to bless others. I no longer reject the idea of being rich, I welcome it with open arms. It is not money that is evil, it is the love of money above all else that is evil.

And speaking of money, we must remember that "scarcity" can come in many other forms. Time, health, willpower, relationships, and judgement can all be impacted by the scarcity mindset. If we are not careful scarcity thinking can seep past just money and invade other areas of our lives as well. We can start to think that there is a limit on many of the things that we want most. "I will never find *that* person that I am looking for," "The housing market is awful—all the good houses are gone," "There simply isn't enough time in the day." All of these thoughts are built upon fear and are more examples of needing to fight the ENEMY. I thought I had overcome most of the scarcity thinking in my personal life and I was surprised to see that it had leaked into my business life. Being in the supplement business, I am keenly aware of the competition and what a saturated market it is. This "awareness" can easily translate into the type of mindset that I've tried to avoid. Recently we reached out to another ecommerce company that was doing quite well and set up a meeting with them in hopes of learning how to increase our sales. We met with Jeff, one of the founders of Bucked Up, and he was willing, almost eager, to share some of the tools and techniques that had helped him grow the business. Through this meeting I realized that our markets overlapped quite a bit and I immediately thought, "Wow, I can't believe this guy is being so generous with his information ... especially with a competitor." I don't know if I would have been that willing to share with someone fighting for the same customers. It was almost as if Jeff could hear my thoughts because in that precise moment he said, "The supplement industry is a billion-dollar industry—there is plenty of room for everyone." Wow, that one will stick with me. Because so often we are trapped into focusing on the competition or thinking of the limited pieces of "pie," rather than remembering, as Jeff did, that there are no limits, only opportunities.

A critical foundational piece for becoming a multiplier is understanding that the pie is a myth. It is suppressing all thoughts of sparsity and insufficiencies and replacing those thoughts with plentitude and prosperity. Each day you have the freedom to choose how you are going to think and what you want to do. This beautiful world of ours is filled with abundance. We must be good stewards. We must cultivate a character of gratitude. But our success in life DOES not take away from the success of others. "There's plenty of room for everyone!" Once you have quieted the voice of scarcity and opened your mind to abundance you will be better prepared to live a life of creating. It is in this place that you will discover the variety of ways that creating can contribute to your life: as an outlet, to fill a void, to help you connect, to help you appreciate, and to ultimately create the energy you need to live your best life.

Sourdough Bread

There are endless ways to create. For most of us, when we think of creativity we think of "the arts." The fine arts like painting, sculpting, or photography. Or maybe the performing arts like music, song, dance, and theatre. I'm a lost cause in every single one of these. Creativity is not one of my strengths. I'm not being falsely modest. My left-brain comes alive with numbers, equations, facts, statistics and planning out my day in half hour increments (seriously). My right-brain however is often shriveled up in the corner and sometimes lets out a plea to not be forgotten. This is how sourdough bread entered my life.

I was in my last year of graduate school, while at the same time trying to help build a brand, be a decent mother, and trying to play nurse to Dan. I could feel myself getting overwhelmed regularly, but when I looked at everything I was juggling there didn't seem to be a ball that I could drop. I needed to find a way to decompress, but truthfully, I don't do "relaxation" very well. I could feel the stress building, with no outlet. One day while trying to unwind, I was scrolling through Instagram (not the recommended way to unwind by the way) and I was intrigued by a post about making sourdough bread. I was actually more intrigued by the bacteria. I did my thesis on the microbiome and I was fascinated by the idea that I could capture bacteria in the air to make my own starter. From what I read, a simple mix of flour, water, and a little patience was all I needed to make a starter from scratch.

So I began.

After seven days my starter was nice and bubbly, and I was ready to make my first loaf. With a few books, a few websites, and the simplest of baking tools, I proceeded. I'll admit that it wasn't a raging success at first. But the results were promising enough to encourage me to keep going. Slowly the loaves got better and better and I found baking to be surprisingly therapeutic. It also served another unexpected purpose. Dan was on chemotherapy at the time and would be left feeling quite ill after each treatment. His appetite was low and all he could stomach was mild food. It is painful seeing someone you love suffer, and I felt so helpless. I badly wanted to help in some way, in *any* way. The bread became that way. He loved the bread, and not only could he could eat it without getting sick, it was something that he could look forward to on chemo days.

It wasn't long until I was baking up a storm. The thing with sourdough is that you need to make a daily decision to either use the fresh starter or end up throwing it away. That was a simple decision for me (waste is of the devil right). So each night before bed I would whip up 2 loaves to let rise overnight and each morning I would bake the bread. The funny thing is that I wasn't even really that interested in eating the bread. It was the process of creating the bread that I found to be so gratifying. To be able to take the most elemental food ingredients and create something delicious and beautiful was so enjoyable.

But I was baking a lot, so I began giving most of the loaves away.

I was a bit awkward at first, "Here's some bread I baked," or, "Hey I thought you might like some warm bread," as I took the loaves to random neighbors. I continued to bake and with each loaf came a growing desire to share it (my kids may have hijacked a loaf or two).

This is when I discovered something amazing.

Little by little I learned something incredible about bread. I've actually never seen anything quite like it. Bread seems to be a universally accepted form of love. A simple, almost primitive, loaf of flour, water, and salt, can extend across almost any social border to simply offer the message of love. Bread can say, "Welcome to the neighborhood," "I'm so sorry your father died," "Thanks for driving my kids last night," "I'm so glad we are friends," "I hope everything is okay," "I heard it was your birthday"... the list could go on and on. It is no wonder to me now that the greatest of all declared Himself "the bread of life".

Warm, freshly baked bread evolved to be not only my outlet for creation, but suddenly it was the means of filling me in ways that I hadn't expected. In my very busy life, I hadn't been taking the time to really connect with anyone outside of my inner circle (which is a big deal being an extrovert). This changed with each bread delivery. Sometimes I would drop off bread and exchange the briefest pleasantries and sometimes I would stay and discuss some of life's deepest challenges with friends and neighbors. Before I started baking bread, I thought I needed less on my plate, but what I discovered was that I simply needed something different. I needed to conceive and construct, and soon I was filled by the simple art of creating and sharing.

A Key Ingredient

There have been times in my life when I have felt a growing dissatisfaction that was hard to identify. A subtle yet pervasive feeling that cast a shadow in my life. I have also seen this same sort of discontent diffuse into the lives of those I care about. The ebb and flow of life is totally natural, but we must be careful to not let times of dissatisfaction permeate our lives too deeply. If we are not careful it can be like a mold that grows in a dark corner and quickly spreads. What was once a problem within ourselves can become a problem in our family, our jobs, or our marriages. Suddenly our entire world just feels "off," or, worse, suddenly we think we need to escape it all. May I suggest that sometimes the solution to this unidentifiable inner dissatisfaction is a simple one. Sometimes all that is missing is a little creativity. Sometimes we look to fill our needs in a myriad of ways without considering the need of creations. This is an area of life that may not seem like a priority, and without the proper attention it can easily be set aside. But I promise you that like progress, your soul also craves creation—in whatever format that is suited to you. Sometimes the emptiness that may need filling in our lives can easily be filled by the power of creation.

195

While not one that is immediately considered, or even highly valued, creation is very much a human NEED.

May I also suggest that a little can go a long way. Please know that this area does NOT need to take up ALL of your time, or even MOST of your time. Since we've been talking about sourdough, we can use natural yeast as an analogy here. Creation can be a lot like yeast. Yeast is a living organism that develops and multiplies within the dough. The mechanism of leavening or causing dough to rise by fermentation of the microorganisms is a slow and quiet process. Over time these living cells disperse throughout the loaf, until every bit of it is affected by the rising agent. Without it, the mixture would never be transformed into a loaf of bread. Like yeast, your life must include some sort of creativity. You may not think that you have the need for creativity, but that is another false assumption. Creation brings happiness which is a need we all have. You don't need a lot, in fact it need not be the primary ingredient, but it is one that is critical nonetheless

Create & Share

If you're not the "creative" type, and trust me I know exactly how you feel, look for a way to create anyway! You may not think that you have gifts or talents, but that simply isn't true. Create a great product, create a cohesive team, and while you're at it, let the team be a part of what you're creating. People are more invested in the things that they help create! Create lasting friendships, create amazing food, create beautiful memories, create love and trust, create safety and security. You don't need money, influence, or power to create, truthfully you don't really even need talent. Everyone can create something of beauty or substance.

I have a friend that has the most beautiful yard! She can name every tree, bush, and flower (both in English and Latin), and you can just FEEL a piece of her heart when you sit in her backyard and see all that she has created. I have another friend that takes the MOST beautiful pictures! She has traveled around the world and has captured stunning moments that can transport you to those exact places with just a glance. I love being in her home and seeing her talent. I have another friend that is so happy! She is always smiling and has the most infectious laugh! It's one of those laughs that the minute you hear it you simply cannot keep your own laugh from joining in the chorus. It seems to flow from her, right into me and I LOVE IT! I am drawn to her if only to hear her laugh. I have another dear friend who is so well versed, and has so much wisdom, that I often feel smarter just by sitting next to him. He freely offers insights and perspectives that fill my mind with wonder. I have learned so much from just listening to his simplest musings. These people enrich my life because they have embraced their gifts and talents. They aren't eager to suppress their uniqueness, but rather they have cultivated it in a way that blesses not only their own lives, but the lives of those that are lucky enough to be around them. I love these types of people. Somehow seeing them master their own creativity, inspires me to listen more deeply to my own.

For those of you who are the creative type and already know exactly what makes your soul sing, once you've found time to create, next look for a way to share it. We are all blessed by the creativity of others. Not everyone will share your passion or appreciate your creations but share anyway! And once you have created, and shared, then is the time to teach someone else. That is the epitome of being a multiplier and is a part of the circle of life. To learn, to create, to share, and to teach. This has been the pattern since the beginning of mankind and is also a pattern that brings joy and purpose into our lives.

I have a daughter and all she wants to be is a mother. She has a Pinterest board just filled with wedding dresses and babies. She's sharp as a tack and has the talent to be anything in this world, and what truly makes her heart happy is the idea of being a mother. So my wish for her is that when she someday has the opportunity to be a mother, that she will create the home that she desires, that she will share her talents and compassion with her children and those around her, and that through her example she will teach her own children what it means to be a mother. My sons will follow a similar pattern, not with motherhood, but with business. Both of my sons are natural entrepreneurs. They each want to learn about business so that they can someday have their own. My hope for them is the same as for my daughters. That along their path they will learn, create, share, and then eventually teach others how to do the same.

Words of Creation

Another powerful tool of creation is words. Your words. I'm not talking about writing poetry or becoming an author. I am simply talking about using words to connect, to heal, to inspire, or to share your story. Along your journey of life you will hopefully see that you are not the only traveler. There are others along your pathway that could benefit from your words. There are feet that need steadying, minds that need inspiring, hands that need holding, and hearts that need encouraging. The incredible things about words is that they have the power to do all of those things. Who needs your words? Words of love, words of praise, words of wisdom, words of leadership? Who needs to hear the things that you have to say? What are the words inside of you that are meant to be shared? The definition of creation is "the action or process of bringing something into existence." Think of how easily you can do this with words. A letter to someone you admire. A journal entry for your posterity where you highlight the things that have shaped who you are. Or simply words combined together to express love or appreciation for another person. Think of all the things that you could create with just words. It is words—not paint, not bricks, not instruments, but words—that have been used to generate some of this world's greatest creations.

Don't underestimate the impact that your words can make on the lives of others. Harriet Beecher Stowe is an example of someone who used her words to produce a work of creation that changed the course of this country. Harriet was born on June 14, 1811 in Litchfield, Connecticut and was educated at an all-girls school. She moved to Ohio where she was married and had seven children. During this time, Harriet became involved with the Underground Railroad which temporarily housed fugitive slaves on their journey to freedom. She became more and more distraught by slavery. In 1850, Congress enacted the Fugitive Slave Act, which forcibly compelled citizens to assist in the capture of runaway slaves. Any blacks determined by law to be more than a certain number of miles from home was automatically considered a fugitive and could be thrown in jail. With little in terms of power or prestige, Harriet used the only weapon she knew how to use. Her words. She wrote a novel titled *Uncle Tom's Cabin* that portrayed the pain and injustice of slavery through the stories she shared.

She described the physical, emotional, and sexual abuse that enslaved people were forced to endure. With her words, she connected slavery to pain, suffering, and injustice. The book was a smashing success and sold over 300,000 copies in the first year. It had a tremendous impact on the sentiments towards slaves and popularized the anti-slavery movement that eventually led to the outbreak of the Civil War. According to legend, when Harriet met Abraham Lincoln in 1862, he said, "So you're the little woman who wrote the book that started this Great War!" to which she replied, "I did not write it. God wrote it. I merely did his dictation."

What if you created something simply for the joy of creation? There are so many expectations that we put on ourselves, and many of us fall into the trap of being people pleasers and trying to live up to others' expectations. What if you set yourself free of all that and took time to just create? Not for anyone else, just for yourself? What if you set aside all fears associated with creating (usually the fear of rejection), and simply listened to what was inside of you? What if you aren't good at it? Create anyway. What if it's already been done? Create anyway. What if it's a waste of time? CREATE ANYWAY! Dieter Uchtdorf said, "As you take the normal opportunities of your daily life and create something of beauty and helpfulness, you improve not only the world around you but also the world within you!"

Create Your Energy

When was the last time you felt invigorated? Truly excited to just be alive. When was the last time you woke up feeling totally excited about the day? What if you had the ability to feel that way every day for the rest of your life? What if each day you had the ability to create the type of energy that you wanted to have all day? Sure, there might be some changes needed to get you there (like managing sleep, diet, and stress), but I truly believe that it's completely within your control to create the type of person that you want to be and that begins with the energy you channel each day.

Another part of becoming a multiplier is learning to craft the skill of taking control of your own energy. Your entire physical body is a bioelectrical machine, filled with electricity, and generating countless electromagnetic fields. This essentially means that you have your own unique "human force field." Nerve impulses run electrical energy signals throughout your entire body, and these create the energy-field around you as well as, the electromagnetic waves that travel away from your body. This means that your energy is something you actually put out into the world. What is really fascinating is that the strongest magnetic fields you create are generated by the activities of your heart and your brain! So use your thoughts and your feelings to channel the sort of energy you want to have each day.

There is negative energy and positive energy. (There are likely people in your life that brighten your day just by seeing them, and others that you avoid because they somehow seem to suck your energy). Being aware which energy you are frequently tapping into will be a powerful tool in how you create your energy. Creating energy can come from both external and internal sources. External energy can come from things like a sunny day, inspiring music, or good company. Internal energy is solely dependent on your ability to be in tune with what keeps you charged, motivated, and positive. This is another skill that takes effort and practice but pays worthwhile dividends. Creating your energy is a lot like a muscle—the more you use it the stronger it gets.

About a decade ago I was curious about the temptations in my life. Trying to take the advice of "always seek correction" (from Skill #5), I thought that I would have a better chance at self-improvement if I had a better idea of the things that were tempting me. At the most basic level, I'll define a temptation simply as something wrong or unwise that I was drawn to. I'm a spiritual person, so I did some self-reflection and a lot of prayer to try and identify what I was tempted by. I'm no saint, but the typical vices of alcohol, smoking, pornography, or cussing really weren't my cup of tea. So what was it? One day the answer came in the most unusual way. I must have been daydreaming but all of the sudden I had uncommon "vision," for lack of a better word. In my mind's eye I could see strips of paper circling around my brain, and on each piece of paper was written a word. I began to read the words as they circled. "Annoyed." "Irritated." "Ornery." "Bugged." "Offended." "Cranky." "Bothered." I then saw what looked like my own hand reach out and grab a paper and place it right on my heart. This continued and I grabbed each one and wore them as a badge on my heart. Each one a medallion of pride. I had earned these and I was going to make them nice and comfortable right there on my heart.

I'll admit I was surprised as I recognized them for what they were. These were my temptations. I had no idea. Well, I suppose that isn't entirely true. I had fully approved of each one of these at different times. I could actually hear myself expressing some of these out loud; "I am so annoyed right now," "Oh my gosh I was so irritated today," or "the kids are just bugging me right now." It was an eye-opening experience and one that allowed me to see that negative energy had seeped into my life. With that in mind, I was better able to channel the kind of energy I wanted to exude.

Create your energy, or rather, create your positive energy. This means focusing your mind and filling it with positive thoughts, feelings, and actions. Don't be fooled by thinking that this is an assignment for first graders. This is a practice that can have a significant impact on your life. One trick I have implemented over the years is wearing an inconspicuous elastic band around my wrist. When I noticed my mind trying to reenact a previous offense, or replaying something that was bringing in negativity, I would simply give the elastic a good flick. This was both a mental and physical reminder that I wanted to make a shift in my energy. I have also set alarms on my phone every few hours. When the alarm sounds, I take a minute to check in with my own energy to make sure it's right where I want to be. Practicing gratitude or doing service for others are also great ways to attract positivity.

I have watched firsthand how different personalities can affect people around them. I have seen how the positive energy from just one person can lift an entire room in a matter of minutes. Conversely, I have seen people left feeling completely winded and almost beat up, simply by the presence of someone charged with negative energy. Strive to be the former. Seek the good and attempt to surround yourself with inspiring things that spark your positivity. Pay attention to the media you consume, the people you spend time with, the shows that you watch, the music you listen to, the literature you read, even down to the things that you eat. All of these things can have an impact on the energy you create. Imagine being so skilled at channeling positive energy that you could create a palpable change, not only within yourself, but also in others!

Your Greatest Creation

Creation takes not only action, but it also takes decision. The fear of stumbling, the fear of criticism, or the fear of making the "wrong decisions" can be powerful enough to cripple people into inaction. You must fight against that fear! I love the wisdom given by Teddy Roosevelt:

"It is not the critic who counts; not the man who points out how the strong man stumbles, or where the doer of deeds could have done them better. The credit belongs to the man who is actually in the arena, whose face is marred by dust and sweat and blood; who strives valiantly; who errs, who comes short again and again, because there is no effort without error and shortcoming; but who does actually strive to do the deeds; who knows great enthusiasms, the great devotions; who spends himself in a worthy cause; who at the best knows in the end the triumph of high achievement, and who at the worst, if he fails, at least fails while daring greatly, so that his place shall never be with those cold and timid souls who neither know victory nor defeat."

Remember how at the beginning of this chapter, I told you that creativity wasn't one of my strengths? Well, I've learned that creativity can come in places you would never expect. You can create more love, more light, more wisdom, more happiness, more joy, and more laughter. The skill is to simply create something that didn't exist before. Creating can be ANYTHING. But your biggest contribution, your greatest creation, will be the life that you create for yourself. And when you have found that happiness, you will be able expand your energies for purposes far larger than just yourself.

Figure out how you want to contribute to the world and then do it. You have the power to create the life of your dreams. Once you have stepped on the path of creating the life that you want, you can't stop there. It will require choosing and re-choosing every single day. There is such power in agency and knowing that you are living the life that you chose. It takes all of the responsibility and it places it squarely on your shoulders. Yes, it may seem exhausting, but it is one of the most empowering principles that you will ever encounter. You are responsible for your own happiness. You are responsible for the life that you lead. So every single day you need to choose it.

If you have decided to be a parent, then be the very best parent you know how to be. On your hardest days, remember that deep down this is what you really wanted. And then re-choose and recommit. The same idea goes for relationships. If you have decided to create a lasting, committed relationship, then give it your all and create the best relationship you can. This principle applies to anything you want in life. If you want to be the best salesman in the world, then put in the work and realign yourself with that desire every day. Creating a life of meaning and purpose comes from aligning your heart with your behaviors! And then repeating it over and over.

This chapter, and ultimately this book, is about creating the life that you want for yourself. A life that will exhilarate you and have you eager to jump out of bed each morning. There are no quick fixes, no programs, no boxes to check, and no one-size-fits-all when it comes to happiness. You must create it. The idea is a simple one. Take something and make more out of it. The sky really is the limit. The world is your canvas and YOU get to be in charge of what you create with it. Look for the opportunities that are all around you. Add your own secret touch and use the tools and resources at your disposal to become the person that you want and create the life that you desire. The greatest gift you can offer the world, your greatest achievement, will be a life well lived. A life of love, service, kindness, and contribution. May God grant you a glimpse as to why you are here, the wisdom to pursue that path, and the courage to forge ahead boldly.

Practical Tools to Become A Creator:

1. **Check your mindset.** Take some quiet time to really evaluate how you think. Ask yourself some clarifying questions. Are you more of a Multiplier or a Diminisher? Do you tend to think with a scarcity mindset, or are you eagerly abundant in your approach? Is fear a large contributor to your decision making? Do you consider creation an important part of your life? How do you feel about sharing the things

that you create? The ultimate goal is to move our minds away from scarcity and fear, to a place of abundance and creation.

2. **Start Small...just start.** You don't need a canvas, a pen, or a knitting needle to create (although those are all great options). Find something. Anything. What sorts of things are you drawn to? If you like to read, create a book club. If you like business, create a mastermind group. Sports? Create a team, event, or coaching program. There really are no limits. Something as simple as improving and making your surroundings orderly and beautiful is a form of creation.

3. **Create Space.** One of the best ways to get your creative juices flowing, is to have a designated place to work and create. For me this was a very tiny section of our master bedroom that we walled off so that I could have my own private space. This could be a closet, a section in the garage, or even a spot in the attic. Just somewhere that is designed for solitude and inspiration. You might be surprised by your inner creations when you make space for them.

4. **Go to a "Paint Night".** You can usually find these in any town. I still remember the first one I went to. With an empty canvas and a talented instructor, I was in complete shock of what I

created that night. I took my painting home and my kids didn't believe that I had painted it. Truthfully, I hardly belicved it myself. But what was more impressive to me than the painting was the satisfaction that I felt from creating it. So if you are feeling like the right side of your brain needs a little dusting off, then hire someone to help guide you through the creation process. A cooking class, a dance class, a guitar lesson ... anything will do!

5. **Write Something...anything**. Start a journal. Send a letter. Write a thank you card. Begin writing your life story. Others can learn from where you have been. Somehow use words to begin a journey of creation.

Final Thoughts

This life is not a dress rehearsal. We get one shot to become who we want to become. Too many people are going through life on cruise control. They are living in a fog, and simply going through the motions. I wish I had all of the answers - all wrapped up in a tidy little manuscript. But the truth is that only you know what you want. Only you know the areas of your life that bring you such satisfaction that you need only to figure out how to do them "more". Only you know the activities that you should stop doing because they are not adding any meaning to your life. Only you know the people that you need to interact with differently. Only you know the people for whom your influence matters the most. Only you can be the captain of your ship!

I began this book with an assumption that everyone wants to be happy, and I conclude it with the same assumption. I truly believe that each of us has it within our OWN power to find joy and happiness. As you stay focused and fearless, I believe that the skills in this book with help you to find that happiness.

I have been blessed to travel and see a few of the diverse and wonderful places in this beautiful world. I have seen different countries and different cultures and it has shown me just how unique we all are. Each of us is filled with our own individual set of gifts and talents that can be used to lift and inspire others. My hope is that you have discovered some of those talents and are continually in pursuit of the potential that lies within you.

Many of us yearn to make a difference in this world, but the scale of that influence need not be overstated. Simply by being your greatest self, and living your purpose, will elevate you to a place that will positively affect those around you. This world, maybe more than ever, needs your strength, your vision, your wisdom, your connection, your leadership. Double down on whatever you do in the world that's good, that contributes, that raises standards, that lifts values, that inspires people, and that contributes in some way. Our world needs you now more than ever.

You are the author of your own story, and what you write is up to you. The happiness you are seeking won't just *come*, it needs to be created. Never fear the eraser either; editing makes the story better. The whole gamut of human endeavor is open to you. You can become precisely the person that you dream of becoming. There is divinity within you and opportunity all around you. Find your purpose, and go all in. Expect trial and error along the way. Expect that there will be times of uncertainty, and times when your path will not be illuminated. Press forward anyway. Remember that fear and doubt lead to inaction. Know that the life you seek will not come pre-packaged or wrapped with a bow and may not match what you originally envisioned. Keep going anyway. Look to the Master Creator in all things but understand that when it comes to agency and your own life, He looks to be a co-creator and not a dictator. His plan includes creating a magnificent life *with* you and not necessarily *for* you. Trust your intuition, even if it doesn't always make perfect sense at the time. Your journey is to know and understand your *why*. Don't compare the life that you are creating with anyone else. Ever. Their journey is not your journey. You are unique, and the experiences you have had will influence your life in unique ways. Celebrate the differences and allow others to discover their own course. Don't judge. Don't criticize. Offer encouragement and then focus on what you want to create and contribute. Live with intention because how you live is how you will lead. Enjoy the process, be optimistic, and find joy in the journey. You get one shot. Make it great!

Made in the USA
Las Vegas, NV
17 May 2021

23192903R00125